Identity, Social Activism, and the Pursuit of Higher Education

Critical Studies of LATINOS/AS in the Americas

Yolanda Medina and Ángeles Donoso Macaya
General Editors

Vol. 4

The Critical Studies of Latinos/as in the Americas series
is part of the Peter Lang Trade Academic and Textbook list.
Every volume is peer reviewed and meets
the highest quality standards for content and production.

PETER LANG
New York • Bern • Frankfurt • Berlin
Brussels • Vienna • Oxford • Warsaw

MUÑOZ

Identity, Social Activism, and the Pursuit of Higher Education

THE JOURNEY STORIES OF UNDOCUMENTED AND UNAFRAID COMMUNITY ACTIVISTS

PETER LANG
New York • Bern • Frankfurt • Berlin
Brussels • Vienna • Oxford • Warsaw

Library of Congress Cataloging-in-Publication Data

Muñoz, Susana M.
Identity, social activism, and the pursuit of higher education:
the journey stories of undocumented and unafraid community activists /
Susana M. Muñoz.
pages cm. — (Critical studies of Latino/as in the Americas; v. 4)
Includes bibliographical references.
1. Illegal aliens—Education (Higher)—United States. 2. Illegal alien children—
Government policy—United States. 3. Illegal aliens—United States.
4. Identity (Psychology)—United States. 5. Youth—Political activity—
United States. 6. Students—Political activity—United States.
7. Social action—United States. 8. Youth movements—United States.
9. Educational equalization—United States. I. Title.
LC3727.M86   378.19820973—dc23   2015009638
ISBN 978-1-4331-2558-4 (hardcover)
ISBN 978-1-4331-2557-7 (paperback)
ISBN 978-1-4539-1533-2 (e-book)
ISSN 2372-6822 (print)
ISSN 2372-6830 (online)

Bibliographic information published by **Die Deutsche Nationalbibliothek**.
Die Deutsche Nationalbibliothek lists this publication in the "Deutsche
Nationalbibliografie"; detailed bibliographic data are available
on the Internet at http://dnb.d-nb.de/.

Cover photos by Steve Pavey and the National Immigrant Youth Alliance (NIYA),
taken in 2011 (Atlanta) and 2012 (Portland)

The paper in this book meets the guidelines for permanence and durability
of the Committee on Production Guidelines for Book Longevity
of the Council of Library Resources.

© 2015 Peter Lang Publishing, Inc., New York
29 Broadway, 18th floor, New York, NY 10006
www.peterlang.com

Printed in the United States of America

Table of Contents

Dedication   vii
Foreword, Stella M. Flores   ix
Acknowledgments   xv

Chapter One
   Introduction   1

Chapter Two
   Undocumented Journey–Stories of Migration, Family,
   and Schooling: Participant Profiles   19

Chapter Three
   College Access and Experiences in Higher Education
   for Undocumented Students ... *"Why did they recruit
   us, if they aren't going to support us?"*   37

Chapter Four
   Unpacking the "Staying In" and "Coming Out" Process
   ... *"Yeah, it's kind of funny because every time I tell someone
   I don't have papers, they're like, 'No way, are you serious?'"*   55

Chapter Five
  Social Activism and Defining "Undocumented and
  Unafraid" ... *"After years of feeling powerless, feeling
  ashamed, and feeling afraid and to see people who have
  that courage and conviction to do something"*   71

Chapter Six
  Cultivating Undocumented and Unafraid as a Form
  of Resistance to Legal Violence ... *"We fight, sometimes,
  for single issues, but as human beings we aren't single issues"*   93

Chapter Seven
  From Undocumented to Becoming DACAmented ...
  *"I licked my card and it tastes like plastic, it doesn't
  taste like freedom"*   113

Chapter Eight
  Conclusion   125

Bibliography   135

Dedication

Este libro es para los activistas indocumentados que se encuentran en toda la nación, quienes inspiran, actúan buscando el cambio y comprometerse a luchar contra las injusticias detrás del sistema inmigratorio. Sus voces son necesarias, importantes y muy valiosas.

For the undocumented immigration activists in this book and across the nation, who inspire, agitate, infiltrate, and interrogate the injustices of our immigration system. Your voices are needed, important, and valued.

For Julisa and Mirely.

Foreword

STELLA M. FLORES

In January 2015, the American Association of State Colleges and Universities (AASCU) released its list of top ten higher education state policy issues for the year (AASCU, 2015). The issue of undocumented student college access—the provision and retraction of in-state resident tuition policies, or state DREAM Acts—ranked fifth on that list. Currently, 18 states and multiple private institutions now offer in-state tuition resident policies while 6 states actively prohibit either the tuition break or ban enrollment for undocumented students at public colleges and universities. While the progress for educational equity has been slow, the mere recognition of the educational trajectories of undocumented students represents a remarkable sign of public notice on this issue as it has now penetrated the most critical policy venues for higher education in the United States. President Obama's Deferred Action for Childhood Arrivals (DACA) and the most recent Executive Action proposals have provided a national spotlight for the state DREAM Act policies at a level not previously seen by the current generation. The central question for these state and federal policy initiatives is whether these opportunities will be sustained and how these policy changes in legal status affect students and their families.

The Migration Policy Institute estimates that 1.75 million unauthorized immigrants who were brought to the United States as children, meet the DACA specific criteria allowing them to be eligible for deportation relief under this initiative (Batalova & Mittelstadt, 2012). Approximately 72 percent of this potentially eligible group is currently high school age or above, with another 28 percent reaching this age soon. The states with the highest proportion of likely DACA-eligible students are California, Texas, Florida, New York, and Illinois, states that all have a form of a state DREAM Act. The five states with the next largest estimated number of DACA-eligible students are Arizona, New Jersey, Georgia, North Carolina, and Colorado, most of which have formal bans prohibiting the enrollment of or granting of in-state tuition to undocumented students with the exception of New Jersey and Colorado.

In the interim, dozens of scholars have produced research from various disciplines using multiple methods to investigate the status of undocumented students seeking to attend college. The policy analysis research to date is remarkably clear on one outcome—students likely to be undocumented and Latino who live in states with a state DREAM Act are more likely to enter college than similar students in states without this policy (Flores, 2010a, 2010b; Kaushal, 2008). Flores and Horn (2009) found that state DREAM Act beneficiaries are as likely to persist in college through to completion at a selective public institution as compared to similar students who are U.S. citizens. Still, states continue to legislate bans barring higher education opportunities for these students or in some cases rescind the state DREAM Acts altogether (e.g., Wisconsin). By the time this book goes to press, the Texas state DREAM Act may no longer be in existence.

In the midst of policy wins and loses, however, the student story is often lost in policy analysis literature. Professor Susana Muñoz provides an exquisite and rigorous portrait detailing a more profound understanding of how undocumented individuals make meaning of their legal status within the contexts of higher education and social activism. The state DREAM Acts did not legislate themselves out of boredom or sheer good will. Activism, sacrifice, community mobilization, and the act of "outing" oneself were actions at the forefront of the last decade. Undocumented student activism has been on the rise, and the stories of these actions will finally be thoroughly explicated with this book.

Muñoz's work poignantly uses student voices to offer a compelling argument for making the topic of immigration a civil rights issue. An outcome of this book is that it challenges the current public discourse painting undocumented students solely in terms emphasizing their "life in the shadows," but instead examines the various methods that undocumented students use to access and succeed in higher education, despite not having legal status and without access to federal and state financial aid.

Identity, Social Activism, and the Pursuit of Higher Education: The Journey-stories of Undocumented and Unafraid Community Activists focuses on the process through which undocumented college students grapple to find meaning with their identities, with college persistence, and in their lived experiences under the curtain of anti-immigration legislation. Employing Chicana feminist scholarship and critical methodologies, Professor Muñoz weaves student narratives with complexity; examining how undocumented students make meaning and intellectualize their legal status and their roles as social activists. The narratives in this book are raw and inspirational. She offers rich texture and critical perspectives to the process of disclosing one's legal status and introduces the concept of *critical legal consciousness;* an awareness that these social activists use to gain new knowledge about their legality. Professor Muñoz challenges scholars, policymakers, and higher education practitioners to take more inclusive approaches to the intersections of difference and of identity that are intertwined in undocumented students' legal status as well as other salient social identities. The narratives shared in this book offer insights into how critical legal consciousness can be used as a tool to critique policies that directly affect undocumented students, such as the DACA policy.

This book is an enriching exploration of identity and persistence and heartbreak. It is also a book about a scholar's earnest commitment to reshaping the public discourse on undocumented students by sharing her heartfelt authenticity and vulnerability as a scholar. There are few opportunities within critical scholarship to delve deeply into a researcher's background and personal plight in order to not only shed light on one of the most controversial topics of our time but also to understand how background and experience influence one's relationship with the research. This book invites us to reimagine the ways in which our colleges and universities can demonstrate inclusivity, equity, and justice but also to identify when policy and practices can harm and further silence the voices of undocumented students. As a policy analyst, the work of Professor Muñoz strengthens the field of immigration and civil rights research. She completes the circle of experience and documentation with her empirical work as well as her own story. I encourage a reading of these case studies as they ground the work of all scholars of immigration and education and provide an understanding of a critical student experience in U.S. schools from kindergarten to college completion.

Stella M. Flores
Associate Professor of Public Policy and Higher Education
Vanderbilt University
Nashville, TN

References

American Association of State Colleges and Universities. (2015). Top ten higher education state policy issues for 2015. Washington, DC: American Association of State Colleges and Universities. Retrieved from: http://www.aascu.org/policy/publicati ons/policymatters/Top10StatePolicyIssues2015.pdf

Batalova, J., & Mittelstadt, M. (2012). *Relief from deportation: Demographic profile of the DREAMers potentially eligible under the deferred action policy.* Washington, DC: Migration Policy Institute.

Flores, S. M. (2010a). State "dream acts": The effect of in-state resident tuition policies on the college enrollment of undocumented Latino students in the United States. *The Review of Higher Education, 33,* 239–283.

Flores, S. M. (2010b). The first state dream act: Immigration and in-state resident tuition in Texas. *Educational Evaluation and Policy Analysis, 32,* 435–455.

Flores, S. M., & Horn, C. L. (2009–2010). College persistence and undocumented students at a selective public university: A quantitative case study analysis. *Journal of College Student Retention, 11,* 57–76.

Kaushal, N. (2008). In-state tuition for the undocumented: Education effects on Mexican young adults. *Journal of Policy Analysis and Management, 27,* 771–792.

Acknowledgments

Words cannot express the gratitude that I hold for the many individuals in my life who made writing this book possible. First and foremost, I am forever indebted to the community activists who participated in this project. Your stories, your lives, your wisdom, your activism have gripped my heart, my spirit, and my consciousness. I am a different scholar because of your work and the lives you lead. You all truly embody virtues of beauty, justice, and empowerment, which have inspired a nation to act.

Over a year ago, after my AERA conference presentation, Yolanda Medina from Peter Lang approached me about the possibility of writing this book. I was terrified at the thought of tackling such a monumental feat as an untenured professor. Thank you, Yolanda, for your unwavering support and advice. You have helped me in ways in which you will never know.

I am grateful to have a group of academic mentors who always make time to lend their wisdom and advocate on my behalf. Thank you to Drs. William Perez, Laura Rendón, Marybeth Gasman, Stella Flores, Robert Teranishi, Nana Osei-Kofi, Rene Antrop-Gonzalez, Larry

Ebbers, Kristen Renn, Dafina-Lazarus Stewart, and Cecilia Rios Aguilar. The book process did not come to fruition without a healthy dose of self-doubt, anxiety, and stress but I am thankful for a group of academic women who I have the pleasure of calling my "sistah-scholars." To my fabulous sistah-scholars, Dras. Michelle Espino, Judy Marquez Kiyama, and Liliana Garces, you have uplifted me in my darkest moments and celebrated all my small victories. I feel continuously blessed to have you all in my life and am thankful to you for allowing me to be my authentic self. I am so appreciative of all your love and support.

I am also inspired by the work of community activists, graduate students, and academic friends who have dedicated much of their time and research to the undocumented immigrant community. I am thankful for Nancy Guarneros, Laura Bohórquez Garcia, Matt Matera, Angela Chen, Christopher Ramirez, Cyndi Alcantar, Edwin Hernandez, Jessica Valenzuela, Fanny Yeung, Genevieve Negron-Gonzales, Kenny Nienhusser, Blanca Vega, Will de Pilar, Noe Ortega, and Susana Hernandez as well as organizations such as ScholarshipsA-Z, United We Dream, National Immigration Youth Activist, Queer Immigrant Undocumented Project, Culture Strike, UndocuScholars (UCLA), and the National Forum for the Public Good (University of Michigan). I know the world is better because of the outstanding work that you all do every day. I also want to recognize two remarkable graduate students who made this book writing process possible. Thank you, Gabriel Chaparro, not only for your friendship but also for taking on the task of correcting all the technical writing in this book. Amber Tucker, thank you for all your assistance with coding and for taking time to listen to me process through themes, chapters, and topics for this book.

I would like to acknowledge the Institute for Excellence in Urban Education (IEUE) for funding this project and to my colleagues at the University of Wisconsin–Milwaukee for gently asking about my book progress and for providing much needed encouragement. In particular, thank you Drs. Decoteau Irby, Latish Reed, and Regina Smith for your enduring validation and encouragement.

On the home front, thank you to my parents, siblings, my family in Merida, Yucatan, Mexico, and in the U.S., and my sorority sisters in Milwaukee who have been a continuous source of support. I also would like to acknowledge my life partner, Juan A. Rodriguez. Thank you for being a compassionate listener, for your everlasting support of my academic work, and for instinctively knowing when to buy cupcakes in order to lift my spirits. Your love and support serves as a source of strength. Lastly, to the two most important, most intelligent emerging scholar activists, Julisa and Mirely. Being your Mama is the best award that anyone has ever bestowed on me. I hope this book will one day inspire you both to fight against injustices and to change the world.

About the book cover:

The book cover photos were taken by Steve Pavey along with members from the National Immigrant Youth Alliance (NIYA) in Atlanta, Georgia (2011) and Portland, Oregon (2012). These photos illustrate hope as undocumented activists reclaim their dignity within the struggle for human rights. To view more of Steve Pavey's photography please visit his website "Hope in Focus" at http://www.stevepavey.com

Chapter One

Introduction

"We started by shouting. 'No papers, no fear, immigrants are marching here!' And then alongside hundreds of people, we finally chanted loudly and proudly, 'undocumented and unafraid, undocumented and unafraid!" (Ireri Unzueta, Immigrant Youth Activist)

In 2007, I conducted my dissertation research study in the Rocky Mountain region where I met four undocumented Mexican women who were to have a profound impact on my life. During one of my interviews, I remember sitting across the table from Sofi, an outgoing, small-framed college junior studying business administration who hailed from Hueyotlipan, Tlaxcala, Mexico. Our conversations delved into her family life, cultural background, prior schooling, and college experiences. As Sofi discussed her challenges and hardships of navigating her legal status in higher education, I distinctly recall that critical moment in which Sofi let out a deep sigh as she sank back into her chair. Her eyes were focused intently at the ground as she expressed, "Sometimes I feel ashamed when I talk about my status; it makes me want to avoid taking about it." The word "ashamed" struck a chord in my heart; I pursed my lips together and shook my head in sadness while blinking back the tears that seemed determined to appear. Sofi's struggle with shame mirrors what many undocumented immigrants experience in U.S. society.

The years following my dissertation study spurred more social activism from undocumented individuals, from occupying streets and congressional offices, to holding public "coming out" forums such as the one held at Daley Plaza in Chicago, Illinois. As I listened and watched undocumented students with pride loudly proclaim themselves as "undocumented, unafraid, and unapologetic," I began to ask, "How do undocumented individuals arrive at this juncture?" This book focuses on the process by which young adults who identify as "undocumented and unafraid" cultivate and heighten their legal-status consciousness through social activism. The purpose of this book is to offer rich stories of undocumented students as they grapple with disclosure of their legal status, their pathway to college access, the impacts of social activism on their legal status, and how their identities are shaped by the current immigration political climate. I begin this chapter with a brief introduction to the literature of immigration policies impacting undocumented children, young adults, and the undocumented youth social movement.

Exclusionary Immigration Policies

Although crossing the border without documentation is legally considered a misdemeanor, U.S. society regards these actions as being parallel to the most heinous punishable crime one can commit. Americans cannot negate the hundreds of years of racism and xenophobia against immigrants and minoritized populations that serve as a backdrop to contemporary immigration conversations. Understanding that many immigration policies are direct responses to exclusion of certain rights and liberties in U.S. society often centralizes the intersection of race and immigration status. Historical exclusionary policies such as the Chinese Exclusionary Act of 1889, a Supreme Court decision, excluded the immigration of individuals of Chinese descent from entering the United States (U.S.). Legal scholars (Orgad & Ruthizer, 2010) contend that even more than 120 years after the Chinese Exclusionary Act, racial categories continue to shape immigration polices by positioning the immigrant subject as either "desirable" or "undesirable." This claim insinuates that race-neutral immigration policies do not exist. In fact, immigration policies systematize stratification of racial populations by answering the question, "Who belongs in the U.S. and who doesn't?"

Anti-immigration policies such as Arizona's Senate Bill 1070 and Alabama's House Bill 56 further criminalize undocumented immigrants for earning a living, driving, or trying to obtain an education. While the intention of these anti-immigrant policies is to create an environment so toxic and unbearable that undocumented immigrants would leave the state and country (self-deportation), these polices have had the opposite outcome. In Alabama, undocumented immigrants initially did leave their homes only to return weeks later after the bill caused unintended consequences. These negative consequences came about when prominent immigrant German and Japanese auto manufacturing representatives were detained for a traffic violation and did not have proper documentation. The thought of potential loss of economic prosperity and the pushback from the business sector caused one Alabama community to rethink their stronghold stance and subsequently revise their policies. The bill also impacted local churches, which essentially made going to soup kitchens and attending Spanish mass a criminal act (Sarlin, 2013). The damage caused by these anti-immigrant policies leaves a lasting impact on the immigrant community. A culture of fear permeates throughout, discouraging undocumented immigrants from seeking assistance or reporting crimes inflicted on themselves or on others. Even U.S.-born children of undocumented immigrants defer higher education, fearing deportation of their parents (Sarlin, 2013). These actions are reminders that when states pass dehumanizing, inhumane, and unjust laws and policies targeting immigrants, the maltreatment of these individuals becomes justified, legitimatized, and normalized through these policies.

Education Policies and Undocumented Youth

The maintenance of a cultural and racial homogeneity has been central to many anti-immigration policies and laws. The plight of educational access for undocumented students was brought to the national spotlight during the *Plyler v. Doe* (1982) Supreme Court ruling. This case decided that K–12 schooling for undocumented children was a fundamental right, citing illiteracy as a detriment to the fabric of society as one rationale (Olivas, 2012). The rationalization of undocumented immigrants becomes apparent when you invoke meaning behind which persons are intentionally invited to become citizens of the U.S. and which are deemed unacceptable to be incorporated into U.S. society. For undocumented persons of color, citizenship has been positioned as a barrier rather than an opportunity (Olivas, 2012). Although *Plyler v. Doe* (1982) was successful in making K–12 education a fundamental right, rights to higher education access continue on a tumultuous pathway.

The access of higher education for undocumented college students has primarily centered on admissions, in-state tuition access, and financial resources. The notion of higher education for undocumented students became public during the Leticia "A" case, which gave undocumented immigrants in-state tuition in California. However, the tuition benefit was overturned in 1994, which coincided with California's Proposition 187, a proposed bill to end all public state benefits to undocumented immigrants. The Illegal Immigration Reform and Immigration Responsibility Act of 1996 (IIRIRA) gave the states responsibility to enact their own statutes and policies around higher education benefits to undocumented students. In 2001, Texas was the first state to pass in-state tuition policies and the Development, Relief, and Education for Alien Minors (DREAM) Act was introduced. This bill would have given undocumented students the opportunity not only to attend college and universities with some financial assistance, but also a pathway to citizenship. In 2010, the Senate voted on this bill, which failed to garner support across both political parties ("DREAM Acts," 2010). Without federal action, states have taken it upon themselves to act on behalf of undocumented students by passing state-sponsored DREAM Acts (i.e., Texas, California, and Illinois), which can offer undocumented students in-state tuition, some state financial aid, but no path to citizenship. The cost of in-state tuition is still considered hefty for families from the lowest economic brackets, but does offer "relief" in comparison to the price of out-of-state tuition. In-state tuition cracks open the door to higher education but providing state and institutional aid is an opportunity to swing the doors wide open. If colleges and universities are truly interested in cultivating an institutional climate inclusive of students without legal status, then they need to provide retention services and hire full-time professional staff privy to issues impacting undocumented students. To date, 18 states offer in-state tuition. On the other end of the spectrum, states including Georgia, Alabama, and South Carolina employ state policies that prohibit undocumented students from enrolling in higher education.

One small "victory" providing undocumented youth some relief was the Deferred Action for Childhood Arrivals (DACA), enacted by President Barack Obama during the summer of 2012. DACA provides eligible youth the ability to gain a work permit and to defer deportation for a consecutive two-year period. Since DACA's inception, approximately 573,704 applications have been received and 430,236 have been approved. These numbers signify that only about half of DACA-eligible recipients (800,000) have been approved for work permits (Gonzales & Terriquez, 2013). The National UnDACAmented Research Project (NURP), coordinated by professors Roberto Gonzales and Veronica Terriquez, reports an increase in economic and social incorporation among young adult DACA recipients. Additionally, DACA recipients reported opening bank accounts, finding a new job, and obtaining a driver's license and a credit card. These milestones signify the ability to experience life alongside the rest of the American population. While DACA is not the silver bullet that will suffice the 11.7 million undocumented immigrants residing in the U.S., it offers a taste of what "living" out of the shadows resembles, all while continuing to live without legal status. The next section of this chapter introduces the framing of my research. I discuss literature on social activism and legal consciousness, which explains the context and the process of how undocumented activists make meaning of their legal status.

The Undocumented Youth Movement

Walter Nicholls's (2013) seminal book, *The DREAMers: How the Undocumented Youth Movement Transformed the Immigration Rights Debate*, points out and discusses the idiosyncrasies associated with the political ideologies and strategies of the immigration rights youth movement. The failed DREAM Act legislation ignited a nationwide wave of community organizing and demonstrations by undocumented youth and their allies. The youth within the immigrant organizations found refuge and a sense of solidarity among the sea of undocumented youth who shared similar realities and struggles. Undocumented youth no longer felt alone with their thoughts of hopelessness and despair, but rather found empowerment and an instant connection to a world that enabled them to use their voices and talents and make claims for justice and human rights. Coming out of the shadows and creating a space within the political sphere caught the attention of the nation. As Nicholls (2013) states, "Their messages, talking points, and emotional stories stress the most strategic qualities of the group, silencing those other aspects that may distort their central messaging" (p. 11). Those other aspects, which Nicholls refers to, are the toxic stigmas or controlling images of immigrants used to criminalize and vilify this population. Instead, youth activists attired in cap and gown stress their allegiances to the U.S., citing their academic accolades, a sense of belonging, and "through no fault of their own" (p. 127) were brought to the U.S., as they continue to contemplate their future plans in the midst of the anti-immigration policies. In his most recent article (2014), he contests that DREAMers, along with popular discourse, have carved out a particular category or "niche" for themselves which positions them as "deserving" undocumented immigrants as opposed to "undeserving."

The suicide of Joaquin Luna from Mission, Texas, which captured national attention, exemplifies the dark realities for undocumented students who are coping with stress and hopelessness because of their legal status (Barrera, 2011). The process of "coming out" provided youth with an opportunity to reclaim their dignity, humanity, and personhood. This proclamation is a way in which youth create communities of solidarity, disseminate knowledge, and empower others through their own stories. By providing a counternarrative to the "silent," "good" immigrant lurking in the shadows, youth have strategically constructed their own compelling messages, highlighting not only their pride in being undocumented, unafraid, and unapologetic, but also how this adopted identity informs and shapes their other social identities such as sexual orientation. This process illustrates that undocumented students are not single-issue individuals and that their legal status is only one aspect of a complex identity that makes them a whole human being (Nicholls, 2013; Seif, 2011).

Legal Consciousness

The term "identity development" is a fluid process in which individuals come to know who they are, but I also argue that it is an umbrella term that includes their worldviews and epistemologies. These activists did not choose to be undocumented, yet their bodies, their mere existence, are contested and politicized by the curtain of immigration dogma.

Chicana scholar Francisca Godinez proposes three different elements using critical race theory and Latina/o critical theory, which considers the structural, political, and representative dimensions of U.S. society, such as policies impacting all facets of lived experiences. Studies on college student identity development have stemmed from traditionally established, dominant culture, and the male student population, which warrants a more critical and nuanced examination of how college student identity development is constructed within the context of college students and higher education. Scholars Torres, Jones, and Renn (2011) contend that previous identity models have simplified the ways in which identity is constructed and only account for psychological and external influences without including complicating multiple contexts as well as the social construction of facets of identity. Research

(Abes, 2009; Abes, Jones, & McEwen, 2007; Jones & McEwen, 2000) has also pushed away from examining identities as individual silos or linear processes and acknowledges the multiplicity and intersection of identities within sociohistorical and sociopolitical contexts. Put another way, identity development is fluid, contextualized, and constructed by how one's identity is influenced, validated, or silenced within a particular environment. An undocumented student understands her/his legal status based on the navigational processes and experiences that place that legal status under a magnifying lens. Identity is also shaped by critical moments in which an individual experiences a life event that ignites reflection on whom she/he chooses to be.

The notion of "legal consciousness" illuminates the understanding of how individuals without documentation function in everyday life "with the law ... or against the law" (Abrego, 2011, p. 360). How undocumented students in higher education navigate resources and individuals on a college campus may be dependent on how they have intellectualized and internalized their legal consciousness. For instance, Gonzales's (2011) work on the transition into adulthood documents the experiences of undocumented youth who face educational, economic, and social limitations that diminish their likelihood of fully participating in the fabric of society. How individuals become aware of their legal status becomes more apparent when individuals start to make future plans for college or employment (Gonzales & Chavez, 2012). The concept of legal consciousness within the discourse of student identity development is impacted by the psychological consequences of anti-immigration policies. The idea of "illegality" is a socially constructed image, which places immigrants as marginalized individuals based on the fluid interpretation of immigration laws. Thus, it is imperative to unpack the construct of "illegality" as a socially, legally, and politically nuanced practice, which reproduces and maintains systems of inequity in contemporary society (De Genova, 2002; Muñoz & Maldonado, 2010). As educators, we need to be privy to the complexities associated with how undocumented students develop their legal consciousness (Abrego, 2011) and what role their legal consciousness plays in their daily actions or inactions within educational, social, and political contexts.

It is also important to note that the construction, or meaning-making, of legal consciousness can depend on the age at which the immigrant arrived in the U.S. For example, Abrego (2011) found first-generation immigrants were most paralyzed by fear, whereas their 1.5 generation counterparts reported stigma as a barrier to claims-making and found that overcoming stigma by this population was more apparent among high-achieving college youth.

William Pérez's (2011) influential book, *Americans by Heart: Undocumented Students and the Promise of Higher Education*, reports that undocumented students in his study valued education, which often manifested as high self-esteem and self-confidence. Additionally, witnessing injustices within their communities and families prompted many undocumented students to participate in civic engagement and social activism. Involvement in these activities allowed undocumented students to develop a heightened sense of their identity while constructing support networks among their peer group to stand in solidarity with other undocumented students, and to gain important knowledge and awareness of their rights as immigrants. Pérez's (2011) employment of Goffman's social stigma theory sheds light on the process in which students make meaning of their legal status within the immigration sociopolitical context. Pérez points out the many risks and benefits associated with disclosing one's legal status. The students in his study describe that they "revealed their status when it worked in their favor and concealed it in situations where they felt it could be used against them" (Pérez, 2011, p. 27). Strategic negotiations were used in the decision-making process to determine how students choose to "come out" as they feared rejection or other negative repercussions. The strategic negotiations within the coming out process are addressed in this book. The next section discusses the lens that was used to examine the stories and narratives from the participants in this book.

Theoretical Perspectives

I draw from the work of Gloria Anzaldúa (1987), who speaks to the struggle of living in brown bodies while acknowledging that colonization causes conflict between the oppressed and the oppressor. The negotiation of how to reconfigure one's lived realities stems from the struggle, the acknowledgment of one's colonized histories, and the recognition of how economic and political forces propel one to find truths in how people can deepen their understanding of themselves. Through this struggle the individual witnesses the most pain. This is what Anzaldúa calls *la facultad*, the ability to peek into one's soul as one contemplates self-meaning. At first, *la facultad* may be viewed as a "survival tactic," which describes individuals who live in a colonized world but choose to navigate rather than resist. A point of rapture occurs in *la facultad* when one's consciousness opens and experiences are perceived with a deeper understanding. *La facultad* embarks on a journey, which allows individuals to tap into their resiliency and assets in order to heal from the wounds inflicted by the colonizer/oppressor. This rebirth, this act of recreating out of destruction, is how one re(writes) her- or himself into existence, or what Anzaldúa calls the creation of a new mestiza consciousness (1999). The notion of "shifting" remains a constant element when Anzaldúa problematizes the conflict between one's cultural values and the values of the dominant culture. This produces the indigenous term *"nepantla*—a space of tension and a space of possible transformation" (Aleman, Delgado Bernal, & Mendoza, 2013, p. 326). It is the action taken against convergent thinking and shifting toward creating a new terrain or a separate space when one truly discovers the authenticity of her- or himself: the mestiza consciousness. I attempt to parallel the concept of mestiza consciousness development with how undocumented social activists make meaning of their legal consciousness.

Concepts of Resistance

In order to fully understand consciousness development, one must contemplate the idea of resistance. In Chela Sandoval's book *Methodology of the Oppressed* (2000), she unveils previous feminist scholars' failure to address how the understanding of one's self prompts oppositional resistance. Sandoval (2000) encourages us to examine how topography (our place), place in the social order, and cultural realities influence how we come to understand our consciousness. She discusses four feminist phases of oppositional consciousness and forms of resistance: equal rights, revolutionary, supremacist, and separatist. Individuals subscribing to the equal rights philosophy argue that we are all equal under the law, as they demand equity in civil rights. "Aesthetically, the equal rights mode of consciousness seeks duplication politically, seeks integration; psychically, it seeks assimilation" (p. 56.6). The revolutionary form calls for the realignment of how differences are positioned within the social order of society. The revolutionary mode of oppositional consciousness operates beyond the dominant/subordinate powers and seeks to reconstruct realities. In the supremacist form, a "subordinate group understands itself to function at a higher state of psychic and social evolution than does its counterparts" (p. 56.7). And finally, the separatist form is established to maintain a completely separate established social order reality, which enables individuals to exist (Aztlán is an example).

As previously stated in my discussion of mestiza consciousness, the act of understanding self is a constant process of grappling between and among various modes of consciousness. Sandoval's differential forms of oppositional consciousness depict the fluidity and movement among the various forms of opposition. It is not a stage or a phase but rather the motion of weaving in and out of the forms of consciousness brought on by crisis, being at a crossroads, or pivotal life experiences. It also represents the relationship and "the work" on individual self-consciousness that shapes self-agency.

Sandoval's book made me think more deeply about two ideas concerning social movements. One, the way we perform social movement, has much to do with the way we see ourselves congruent with our social realities. I see that the rationale for engaging in social justice work, or our purpose with social activism, stems from lived experiences and from the various influences of our social context. Then, within the movement, individuals are transformed and shaped by how we engage and the actions that are taken. We deepen our consciousness and often reevaluate our intentions, our convictions, and our new realities. With new knowledge comes transformation, leading to a differential form of consciousness. Two, much of the identity development literature fails to address issues of space, place, and time-topography. The notion of cultural topography delineates a set of critical points within which individuals and groups seeking to transform dominant and oppressive powers can constitute themselves as resistant and oppositional citizen-subject" (p. 54.4). Topography reminds me how consciousness development, or the process of consciousness development, is privileged by access to other equity-conscious individuals, organizations, and resources. Much of identity development may focus on the individual process of self-understanding, but as one moves along the continuum of space, place, and time, levels of consciousness are not documented. My hunch is that individuals understand their space and place within the context of social order and time. However, given the current societal and systemic structures of dominance, little attention is placed on the understanding, deconstruction, and meaning-making process effects of social movements. The next section provides an overview of the research study.

Study Overview

The overarching purpose of this study is to develop a deeper understanding of how undocumented individuals make meaning of their legal status within the contexts of higher education and social activism. The methodological paradigm used in this study was constructivist (Crotty, 2003; Patton, 2002), which privileges the belief that identity is a socially constructed product that occurs over a period of time and is shaped by multiple contexts. Such epistemology suggests centering the voices of the participants in all aspects of the research. I chose the constructivist approach because it allows me to examine how undocumented individuals make meaning of their life experiences and how their individual contexts shape how they view themselves. A constructivist approach also acknowledges the process in which participants in this study actively engage with society as a lack of legal status causes them to make and shape themselves and the world around them. Crotty (2003) summarized three assumptions of constructivism: (1) special attention is paid to the construction of meaning; (2) it is based on historical and social worldviews; and (3) meaning usually derives as a result of interaction with a human community.

Methods

Critical qualitative research was employed in my research design, which takes several assumptions into consideration, such as the interrogation of power, how values are mediated by multiple contexts, how language matters in cultivating our awareness, the awareness of privilege across social groups, and the recognition of multiple forms of oppressions (Crotty, 2003). I constructed questions and conducted my analyses to address issues of social justice and equity for my participants. This study contains 39 interviews from 13 undocumented college students and college graduates who self-identified as undocumented and unafraid. The first interview was unstructured, and asked students to discuss their life history. Many of them discussed their journey-stories into the U.S., their schooling experiences, college access, and, most of all, the struggles endured by their families.

The second interview focused on how participants made meaning of their legal identity within the contexts of higher education and social activism. The questions I asked included, "How did you feel about yourself before you came out as undocumented to other people?" "What prompted you to come out about your legal status?" "Tell me about a critical moment during your college process in which you revealed your legal status to someone other than a family member." "What does it mean for you to be undocumented and unafraid?" The third interview presented an opportunity to revisit and gain more depth from the second interview, as well as interrogate them more about their multiple identities with questions such as, "Can you say more about your multiple identities (gender, class, sexual orientation)?" "How has each of your identities formed or changed while in college and in your experiences with social activism, and have you encountered opposition from others?" and "If so, how do you deal with opposition to any of your multiple identities?"

The interview protocol was reviewed and modified by two scholars who research student development theory and identity development. Each individual interview lasted approximately 90 minutes and was conducted via Skype. The audio was transcribed verbatim and the participants selected pseudonyms. The interviews were spread out over a 10-month period. This time span allowed participants time to review the transcripts and it also created time for immigration events to transpire. For instance, the Deferred Action for Childhood Arrivals (DACA) executive order passed in August 2012 and was an opportunity for me to gain insights and form opinions about this policy and how it may impact the identity development of participants.

Participant Selection

A snowball sampling method was employed to identify participants using two methods. For the first method, I sent an email to immigration research scholars, community activists, and higher education administrators requesting that they forward an invitation letter to undocumented youth activists. For the second method, I used 12 DREAM Act alliance organizations across the country, the DreamActivist.org website, and the DREAM Act Facebook page to solicit participants for this study.

The criteria for participant selection required that students: (1) must be publically out and open about their legal status, (2) identify as a person of color, (3) attend college, attended college and have stopped out, or are college graduates, and (4) identify as an activist within immigration issues. This last criterion yielded diversity among localities but the sample is completely of Latina/o descent, which is not representative of the heterogeneity among the undocumented population. The majority of the sample also represents students who came from private institutions ($n = 7$). Only three students represent four-year institutions, two students represent community colleges (one stopped out), and one student was enrolled at Freedom University in Athens, Georgia. Most of the participants in this study obtained the majority of their educational experiences in the U.S., and self-identified as undocumented and unafraid. At the time of the study, seven students were classified as undergraduates, three were pursuing graduate studies, and two students were college graduates working full-time. One student stopped out of community college and is at the time of this writing working with an immigration advocacy group.

My Researcher Standpoint

I remember boarding an airplane but I do not remember the particulars about my destination. I have no recollection about my feelings associated with leaving my country of origin, Yucatán, Mexico. I was just a painfully shy, wide-eyed six years old, who quietly observed her new surroundings in hopes of rekindling old feelings of home. For me, home is hearing the crashing roar of ocean waves against the silky white sandy beaches. Home is hearing a cumbia variation of *balia como Juana la cubana* from the neighbor's radio from down the block. Home is the smells from three different meats (*puchero*) cooking in the same generational *olla* and watching my *tia* spoon out the fat foam that formed around the edges of the pot. "*Tienes que sacar la espuma*" she would say to me. These remnants of home were not part of the fabric of my new home. My new home was not Los Angeles, Chicago, or San Antonio. My new home was Fairbanks, Alaska. My stepfather is Anglo and my mother was my only connection to understanding my home roots. I had lost my language along the way because speaking a foreign language was a reminder that I was different and it was frowned upon in my previous schooling experiences. "She's not going to learn English if she relies on her Spanish to understand her homework," the teachers would say. I loathed my difference during my late adolescence. I had internalized my cultural heritage as a signal that I did not belong. I did not see positive examples of Mexican Americans in my community. I did not like being different. In many ways, my light skin and green eyes aided in my own assimilation to the dominate culture. My returns to Mérida, Yucatán, was another indicator that I no longer belonged as my broken Spanish reflected that I was indeed, *agringada*. I was part of two worlds but belonged to none.

"Where are you from?" was a question from new acquaintances that always evoked a degree of anxiety and tension. I arrived in the United States (U.S.) from Mexico at the age of 6, but was raised in three different states. The question "Where are you from?" began an internal conversation about how much information I should share and how much energy I needed to expend to field questions about my arrival in the U.S. I feared judgment from others and it prompted me to hide my ethnic identity and my immigration story through silence. The stigma associated with being an immigrant or Mexican was a topic I was never ready to address in my formative years.

In my college years, Gloria Anzaldúa's work (1987, 1999) provided me with language to intellectualize my experiences by acknowledging the discursive and constructed influences that reproduce interlocking systems of oppressions contributed to my self-hate. Anzaldúa and other Chicana feminist theorists transformed my own consciousness of self, institutions, and social inequity. I approach my research with these lived experiences and mestiza consciousness (Anzaldúa, 1987, 1999). The participants in this study and I share a "journey-story," which is the act of leaving behind a family, personal mementos, and homeland for new territory. While I share a similar ethnic identity with my participants, their legal status poses a stark contrast to my own experiences. I arrived in the U.S. in the late 1970s on my mother's travel visa and through the assistance of my U.S.-born stepfather, we obtained citizenship status within four years of our arrival. My citizenship privilege not only enabled me to access financial resources and opportunities to further my education, it also allowed me to visit my native country and care for an ailing relative. I never had to think about possible deportation or being separated from loved ones because of my citizenship privilege. Over the past six years, I have spent the majority of my academic life examining the experiences of undocumented college students. While I bring a wealth of prior knowledge to this topic, I am grateful for the undocumented individuals and activists in my life who continually inspire me to walk through life courageously and with purpose.

Organization of the Book

The intentionality behind the organization of the book was vulnerability. I introduce each chapter with a personal reflection that is directly tied to the chapter title. My reflections describe an experience, event, or moment that I encountered while writing this book, or a previous life moment that illuminates the chapter theme. I close each chapter with a final reflection about the findings in it.

The second chapter introduces the participants in this study by providing a short, detailed account of their journey-stories. In Chapter Three, I discuss how students gained information about their college choice, institutional agents of support during the college process, the experiences of graduate students navigating higher education, and how these participants grapple with microaggressions and depression due to their legal status. I discuss the coming out process for undocumented activists in Chapter Four by examining the rationale behind concealing their legal status, how they make meaning from disclosure and the responses from others about their legal status, and how they engage in critical forms of coming out. Chapter Five discusses the parallel of the Chicana/o Movement of the 1960s with the immigration youth movement. I also explain the ways in which social activism is used to empower communities. I problematize the notion of the "perfect DREAMer," and introduce the concept of critical legal consciousness as a way in which activists view legality and activism in critical ways. In Chapter Six, I examine the shortcomings of the foundational college student identity theories and their applicability to undocumented individuals. I present the concept of legal violence and highlight how participants resist legal violence when they self-identify as undocumented and unafraid. I also unveil the complexity and fluidity of identifying as undocumented and unafraid. I focus on the experiences of students becoming DACAmented in Chapter Seven by discussing the ways in which participants use critical legal consciousness to critique this policy. The final chapter provides recommendations for higher education and K–12 entities. I also make recommendations for advancing student development identities and ethical considerations for researchers who study undocumented immigrants. I conclude the book with an open letter to undocumented student activists.

Chapter Two

Undocumented Journey– Stories of Migration, Family, and Schooling: Participant Profiles

I gently tugged on the white cord of my earbuds to release them from my ear cavity and stretch my arms above my head as my hands met in a prayer pose, trying to relieve my body of tension and exhaustion from sitting on my white wooden chair while conducting two back-to-back Skype interviews with participants in my identity study. I let my arms dangle, relaxed my shoulders, and breathed slowly and deeply as I reflected on the past few months of data collection. I stared at my pages of inked notes while I thought back to their journey-stories and muttered the words "too much" under my breath. As young children, had they seen too much? Have we asked them to grow up too fast as they face their lived realities as undocumented immigrants? The background of a journey-story often depicts the people and possessions that were left behind. I feel that these participants bear the heavy burden of carrying the hopes of others along with the pain that was endured during the crossing. They all left a familiar territory, language, and family for a promised better life. Yet, it was during their transition into the U.S. without legal status that they may have witnessed pain and trauma. I inhaled deeply, grabbed the purple ink pen, and wrote the question, "How much struggle and pain can one human endure before they can no longer endure?"

I planned the first round of interviews to be unstructured so that participants had the opportunity to simply understand the purpose of the study and to tell their life histories. I was interested in understanding what prompted their families to leave their country of origin, how their families were initially received by their local context, and about their secondary schooling experiences. Most of the participants were forthright and spoke with comfort, as if telling their story was a natural process; some even asked about my immigration background and why I was studying undocumented students.

The first round of interviews made me ponder two questions: How much pain and struggle can one body endure? Does this make undocumented immigrants resilient people, or does it make the immigration system in the U.S. a terrorist? The experience of living in U.S. society without legal status poses multiple barriers, from inaccessible resources impacting lives to living in shame. Yet, these community activists search for answers and find ways to achieve their goals. They take risks, find opportunities, and question multiple individuals until they are satisfied with a hopeful answer. They hustle, navigate, negotiate, and endure within a system that does not recognize their existence. In this chapter, I introduce these undocumented and unafraid activists by detailing their stories of migration to the U.S., which gives a glimpse into their lives. Following the participant profiles, I conclude the chapter by reflecting on the themes that emerged from their migration experiences.

Activistas de Immigración

From Mexico, **Sarai** is the youngest of the participants to arrive in the U.S. At the age of 3 and as an only child, she has little recollection of living in Mexico and has always regarded the U.S. as home. Her mother has a fifth grade education and her father is college educated with a degree in industrial engineering. Her parents lived in a rural area of Mexico where the education infrastructure was not fully developed. This would have provided Sarai with educational opportunities only through grade school. Her dad lost his job in Mexico as a result of the 1982 economic crisis and that prompted the family to immigrate to the U.S. Her father initially came to the U.S. on a work visa, but because of the immigration process his renewal was delayed. Sarai's legal status was never a point of contention until her family became homeless.

Their attempts to apply for low-income housing were contingent on needing a Social Security number. Sarai also recalls needing a Social Security number to obtain running water; she asks, "How can we access these public utilities that should be accessible to every single person no matter their status, but because we lack the Social Security we can't?" She currently is 18 years old and a freshman at a private college in Pomona, California, and feels "it can be difficult since there are very little number of students who are out (legal status)." Balancing activism work with her studies can be challenging; however, one of her current challenges is to help her parents ease their own fears concerning her activist work. She explains:

> They're very hesitant of me being very active within the community.... . So that's kind of something I still have to deal with. Like I've been empowered, I've been able to help other students come out of the shadows being very vocal, but I haven't been able to necessarily help my parents be vocal and advocate for themselves. So that's something I still have to work on. And it's going to take a very long time because when my parents came here it was very difficult and I was young so I'm not able to remember, and they protected me as much as possible. So they've dealt with a lot of, in situations and instances that were very uncomfortable and were very hard because of their status, so that's something a lot of youth still have to deal with.

Juan is originally from Caracas, Venezuela, and the oldest of three brothers. Juan's parents instilled the value of education in him at a young age. While Juan was in the third grade, Hugo Chávez came into power, which caused the depreciation of the Venezuelan peso. This also prompted Juan's family to curtail much of their spending, which eliminated his private schooling and usual family outings. In 1998, Juan's parents decided to move to the U.S. and the family started to sell off all personal belongings that were not going to make the trek. Prior to moving to the U.S., Juan thought about the movie *Beethoven*, a film depicting family adventures centered on caring for a big family dog. Juan remembered thinking, "This is what America will be like; you have a family house, and you have a bunch of stories. People don't live in apartments. People have dogs in their homes. I had this picture-perfect, cookie-cutter life in my head."

His parents were able to secure L1 visas, which are obtained by professionals who work for companies based in other countries. In Juan's case, his father was working in a company that also had an operating site in the U.S. After the encouragement of other family members residing in the U.S., Juan's family settled in Miami, Florida. At 8 years old, he was enrolled in the third grade and he approached the situation with confidence, stating, "It's time to put to practice what I've learned in private school." Juan quickly endured a tough adjustment to the school system, all while learning a new language, as he thinks back, "I remember coming home crying telling my mom that I didn't want to be in my school, that I wanted to go back because I felt like I didn't fit in school." Owing to his strong adaptability skills, Juan did well in many social circles, was able to use his social networks (friends, peers, counselors), and graduated from high school but suffered a tumultuous college access process trying to secure funding to attend community college. Each semester greeted Juan with an agitated college counselor insisting he show proof of citizenship or the college would rescind financial support. Currently, Juan is finishing his political science degree at a public four-year university in Florida and considering applying to graduate school for further education in public affairs. At the time of his interview, the state of Florida had not passed its in-state tuition.

Yahaira was regarded as a natural-born leader, as she claims, "My mom says that even when I was a kid, I always wanted to help with different things in different ways. So I guess it's just something that comes naturally to me." She is from Michoacán, Mexico, and came to the U.S. in 1992 at age 7. Yahaira came with her mom to join her father. Her mom wanted to reunite their family and to give her daughter better opportunities. She settled with her mom in California, where her mom worked in the fields, a bakery, delivering newspapers, and at a nursing home. Yahaira remembers being very studious. She was not enrolled in ESL courses while in school because her mother advocated against doing so. Yahaira learned English quickly and moved to Kansas City, where she started middle school and graduated from a "predominately school [high school] of color, not particularly well-funded," but she describes herself as "super nerdy, and super involved." "Everyone told me that I was really smart and that I'd be able to do anything and go anywhere and that my life was going to be great and I was going to do wonderful things." She graduated in the top 10 percent of her class but knew that she was unable to attend any of the public colleges because of her immigration status and because the private institutions were "ridiculously expensive." One of Yahaira's high school teachers served as a resource and investigated whether she could adopt Yahaira, whether a citizen could sponsor her, or whether she could return to Mexico and come back. All of her questions led to a brick wall. In the final hour, during the fall after she had graduated from high school, Yahaira heard about a college in Kansas admitting undocumented students. Her college experiences "got complicated and messy"; it took her nine years to complete her bachelor's degree in Spanish. Yahaira's intentions were to teach at the K–12 level, but proof of citizenship is required to take the state credentialing exams. Now Yahaira is self-employed, working with social justice activists and artists.

Antonio is originally from Mexico City, Mexico, and currently attends a private four-year state college. When he was 8 years old, both his parents were abruptly, and without reason, murdered. This traumatic event was the impetus for his immigration to the U.S., to reunite with his older brothers who were already living in there. Antonio's older brother used falsified documentation to bring him to northern Oregon. Antonio describes his first few years in the U.S. as like "carrying a rock." The cultural differences, a new language, and growing up without parents impacted him emotionally. Particularly impacting was not seeing his culture represented in his community, schooling, or among his peers. He first moved to a city in Oregon, which at the time did not have an English as a Second Language (ESL) program; after that, he relocated to a smaller town that was able to provide ESL resources. He admits not caring too much about school and instead focused on sports prior to high school; but his older brothers modeled academic excellence, which motivated him to work hard in school. His counselor nominated him for a scholarship, indicating to him that "you have a story to tell" and was awarded a full scholarship to a private school. Perhaps most interesting about Antonio's story is that he lives in an isolated location, which makes connecting with larger social activist groups difficult. Living in a context in which there is no outlet for a traditional sense of organizing and advocating for immigration rights in large groups has led him to act in small impactful ways to support other undocumented students, and to mentor young boys through sports such as soccer. Antonio knows there are other undocumented students attending his college who recognize the great level of advocacy among the university administration for students without legal status. He is currently majoring in business administration and his hope is to provide his older brother a "retirement" as repayment for raising him.

Jaen was born in Mexico, in the state of Mexico, and moved to the U.S. when he was 8 years old. The stable economy in the U.S. prompted his dad to immigrate first and live in Los Angeles (LA) with family members. As Jaen's mother and sister grew tried of the separation, they moved to LA to reunite the family. Both of Jaen's parents have less than a high school education. His family worked in manufacturing jobs while in Mexico and then they worked in the fabric and garment industry, cutting clothing patterns, while living in LA. Upon entering the fourth grade in LA, Jaen was placed in ESL courses and then switched to bilingual instruction once he moved to New Mexico. "I guess because my reading was at the third grade level as a freshman in high school, I was placed in bilingual classes and that helped out." Jaen's family was influenced by other family members to move to New Mexico because they viewed the state to be more "progressive" and "immigrant friendly." Due to New Mexico's availability of bilingual courses in public schools, Jaen witnessed a vast improvement in his grades. "I needed to be able to communicate with my teachers in Spanish so I could understand them and the material that I was learning." Jaen is a sophomore in business, and a Spanish major at a public four-year institution in New Mexico; he is also involved with the New Mexico DREAM alliance.

Yovany is currently 19 years old and the middle child in his family. Yovany comes from a mixed status family. He first moved to California when he was just 2 months old and later returned with his mother to Mexico, at the age of 5, when his father figure left the family.

His mother faced hardships trying to make a living wage while in Mexico. Then, with encouragement from family members, they returned to the U.S. and settled in Georgia. To sustain the family, Yovany's mother worked multiple jobs and would sleep very little. While he moved around the state of Georgia, he was able to attend school in a predominately white neighborhood. Yovany describes his school as a "Blue Ribbon school, which is top in the nation." Upper-class affluence was clearly apparent in this school's population. While the quality of education was excellent and his teachers "wanted him there mentally," he knew his college options were limited. He graduated from high school in 2010 and worked at a fast-food restaurant for two years before deciding to attend Freedom University, a nonaccredited institution of higher learning for undocumented students. Four faculty members from the University of Georgia founded this university as a means to resist Senate Bill 458. This policy bans undocumented students from enrolling in any of the five selective institutions in the state of Georgia.

David is originally from Michoacán, Mexico, and came to the U.S. when he was in the second grade. David arrived in Tacoma, Washington, after much encouragement from his aunt and uncle who lived in the area. His parents came from a poverty-stricken part of Michoacán where infrastructure, such as roads and schools, were not readily available. His father initially immigrated to the U.S. and sent financial transmittals to David's family. After the family arrived in Tacoma, David's father worked for a wood pallet factory while his mother worked in a laundromat. After two years in ESL, David tested out at the end of the fourth grade. What was most helpful to David was a high school mentoring program, provided by a community center, which paired him with a business leader. This mentor helped navigate questions David had about college support and access. "He would find out information for me about college scholarships and even went with me to my meetings with my counselors." This additional method of support helped David apply for the Melinda Gates Scholarship, which he received and used to fund his college degree at a four-year private school. David graduated from his private college in Washington with a sociology degree and is currently attending graduate school in Chicago, studying community development.

To reunite with her father, **Angelica** came into the U.S at the age of 4 with her mom and brother from Mexico. The family moved between big cities such as Los Angeles and New York until finally making North Carolina their permanent home. Angelica remembers witnessing institutional segregation within the school systems and recounts it as one of the biggest obstacles she faced:

> It was very bizarre because I went to a predominately white middle school and there was a high school down the street and so it was pretty close to where I lived and yet when it came time to go to high school they were sending me to a school that was farther away from my home and it was also where more minorities went to school.

Angelica also critically examined the curriculum of both schools, noticed stark differences between them, and made a conscious choice to attend the school near her home, the school with the best options for college preparation. She asked the Board of Education to be allowed to attend the school closer to her home, but her initial request was denied. Even at 14, her tenacity did not let her quit and she appealed the decision, experiencing her first taste of self-advocacy. Feeling proud and accomplished about winning her appeal, Angelica also felt remorse that others could not benefit from her success. "I feel very sad to think that a lot of people don't know the way the system works and so they can't advocate for themselves or they don't know how to or they may not be comfortable doing so." Even as a hard-working honor roll student in high school, Angelica always feared that her work would not result in being able to attend college because of high tuition costs. Angelica decided on a private Catholic college near her hometown that awarded her a scholarship that provided tuition and fees for four years. She is currently a graduate student studying social work in Chicago at a private college.

Jorge was born in the capital in the state of Mexico. His father was already residing in the U.S. and was trying to obtain a master's degree from Rutgers University. The collapse of the job market at that time in the U.S. and in Mexico resulted in the unemployment of both of Jorge's parents. His uncle became involved with drug cartels in Mexico, putting Jorge's family at risk of violence. "He [his uncle] involved the whole family. We had to move. We didn't have any other choice at this point." At 15, Jorge arrived in Milwaukee on a tourist visa with his family. After that, his family worked at a relative's restaurant and for a cleaning company. He entered high school one grade level behind what he anticipated, and confidently bypassed attending ESL classes because of his English reading and writing preparation while in Mexico. Jorge also had prior knowledge of ESL courses and says, "I heard before that you learn faster in English when you get into the regular classes than ESL, because in ESL you're with people that mostly speak Spanish." He is majoring in construction engineering at a public urban institution and lives with his mom and aunt; his father and sister live in Mexico.

When she was 13 years old, **Jessica** arrived in Tucson, Arizona, from Chihuahua, Mexico, and has been living in the U.S. for nine years. She has very close ties to her sisters and mother. While living in Mexico, she was studious, excelling in math and science courses. Once she arrived in the U.S., she surpassed many of the beginning courses and so exceeded the expectations of her teachers that they questioned her integrity. Jessica remembers, "They [teachers] questioned me, they asked if I copied or if I did my own work." Jessica knew that she had the skills to attend college but challenges were present as she recalls her college recruitment process:

> They tried to recruit me, to find a way for me to go, but they just couldn't do it. I was the asset that they needed for the internship with the top business school, and they couldn't find a way to have me because of Proposition 300.

Proposition 300 prohibits undocumented students from paying in-state tuition or receiving federal or state aid to attend Arizona's public institutions. Jessica considered going back to Mexico to pursue higher education, but the chaos in her previous community prevented her from doing so: "We started to realize that the 'narcos' or the drug cartels in Mexico were killing a lot of people and all the crime started to rise up. So we decided to stay as well because of that reason." Once Jessica decided to pursue higher education in Arizona, one of her Spanish teachers asked her to join a committee to organize an international mariachi conference. Through her involvement, she started to develop more networks and learned of a way to attend community college. Jessica sums her experience: "And little by little I realized that there was a way to be a student at community college... . It's not just like the doors were closed, it was just needing to find a way to get there."

Marco was born in 1990 in Oaxaca, Mexico. His family came from very impoverished conditions and moved to New York when Marco was 3 years old. When asked why his parents chose New York as a destination, he answered, "My parents were fearful of living too close to the border... . Living further from the south made them feel safer." While living in a historically Dominican neighborhood, Marco has noticed an increase in Mexican immigrants in the community over the past ten years. He remembers staying with his maternal grandparents and having to "re-meet" his mother when he crossed the border with his father. Marco also explains that migration experiences were a part of his upbringing. Many newcomer families would gather in his household's living room as his parents explained the nuances of navigating U.S. society without legal status. Marco describes himself as an eager learner who, while in middle school, was recruited to attend a boarding school, which prepares students from low socioeconomic backgrounds for private schooling and college attendance. He was able to receive financial resources to subsidize his tuition but he had to be honest about his legal status because of an internship requirement. Although his boarding school experiences were described as a "culture shock" he says,

> The social capital I was able to gain ... just knowing what private clubs and internships and that whole world of privilege meant and once I went to college, I was just so much more easily able to read all those social cues that I didn't feel uncomfortable with about the affluence because I was already exposed to it.

While counselors where helpful about locating colleges and universities for him to attend, Marco focused his college search on private colleges that were "undocumented student friendly," in terms of their admission policies. Unlike Jesuit schools, the liberal arts private college that Marco chose was not overt about helping undocumented students. He was an active organizer on campus, was able to experience an internship in Washington, D.C., and graduated cum laude with a degree in sociology. He received many accolades for his work as an activist and organizer. "I just have a lot of holistic approach to my art and activism and writing and faith life that it all comes together."

Alex describes his mother: "She's a very powerful woman and she tells me we'd better continue and justice is going to fall on us one day." Alex's mother is his pillar of strength and motivation to fight against injustice. He arrived in the U.S. from Mexico at 16 with a healthy and established queer identity. Alex viewed himself as incredibly intellectual: "I was really good in school. I was ahead of my class by two grades and I remember receiving early admissions to a really good university in Mexico." The middle child (one older brother and one younger sister), Alex considered himself as "middle class" while in Mexico because his parents sold chemicals for cleaning products to national corporations. He attributes the corruption within his father's company as the main motivator for their decision to move to the U.S. While not a big fan of Disneyland, Alex's father informed the family that they were going to visit Disneyland, sold most of their property in Mexico, and moved to California to find work. Alex was faced with many difficult transitions while in the U.S., the most challenging of which was enduring physical abuse from his father. Alex attributes his father's rage to "once being a businessman to flipping burgers and working construction." The continued assaults prompted him, his mother, and younger sister to move out to escape the abusive home environment. "And it's just so funny how politics and justice works because after being in domestic violence, we were supposed to be the ones to get aid, to have some sort of protection. But he ended up playing the system, getting his residency, and his legalization." Growing up in Southern California's segregated

Coachella Valley, Alex had to navigate the multiple identities of others and questioned himself on how to deal with white people, or "how to deal with queer people who don't know anything about immigration." After graduating from high school with a 3.6 GPA, he applied to college, which led him to face another reality of his legal status. The cost of education became much too high; it became a choice of whether to eat, pay for a roof over his head, help his mother, or pay $192.00 per unit at a community college (as opposed to the $20 per unit that his documented counterparts paid). He found his sanctuary in his community and was hired by a nonprofit organization to provide HIV prevention education and contends, "That's where I got my degrees, my certificates, I've got all kinds of education and I realize that I was empowering myself in this process." For Alex, returning to community college is unrealistic because of the high cost, but he reveals, "I opted to do the best I can outside of school to achieve a higher education." Although Alex is not currently in college, his community involvement and commitment to educating his community are testaments that colleges and universities are not the sole venues for obtaining knowledge and empowerment. In fulfilling his mother's wishes of fighting for justice in the community, Alex pays the debt he feels is owed for his mother's sacrifices and the pain she has endured.

Ariel remembers as a 10-year-old the move to the U.S. from Michoacán, Mexico, as being abrupt. He remembers his mother waking him up in the middle of the night to visit his grandmother, who he considered a second mother. They arrived to a tearful outpouring by his relatives as they said their good-byes to Ariel, who did not understand then that he would never see his grandmother or his favorite cousin again. His family lived in a rural area in Mexico where opportunities for employment and education were scarce. His dad had immigrated to the U.S. to an agriculturally rich segment of southeastern Washington three years earlier; therefore, reuniting the family was the reason for the emotional good-byes at Ariel's grandmother's house. Ariel recounts his experience of having to cross the border without his family:

I didn't know anything about borders. I didn't know what the United States, or what it was, what it meant to travel internationally. So I crossed over the

border without proper documentation. I had to pretend that I was the son
of somebody else's mom, a lady who pretended to be my mom. She told me
what to say, what not to say.

Ariel arrived in San Francisco and was reunited with his father and
brothers; they waited three years until his mother could successfully
cross the border to move to Washington State. Ariel spent only four
months in ESL classes and excelled in school. By the time he was in
high school, Ariel was placed in Advanced Placement courses. With
regard to the racial make up of his friends, Ariel noted, "I really spent
most of my class and academic time with white kids, to put it that way.
About a third of my high school was Hispanic. Even at the start of high
school I really didn't hang out with Mexicans or Latinos as much, even
though they were a third of my school." Racial tension was apparent in
Ariel's high school, as he was the only Mexican youth in his classes. He
remembers instances in which he was teased by other Mexican classmates for studying too much and often felt "tokenized" by both white
mentors and Latina/o friends and family. "I mean, there was always
comments to me about 'you should get more of your Mexican friends
to do as good as you' or 'you should be the example.' So even my own
community they used me as 'he is doing it, you guys should do it too.'"
This presented Ariel with an interesting racial dynamic to endure in
addition to navigating his legal status. He went on to complete one
year at the public state college before completing his degree in sociology at a private liberal arts college in the state. He is currently attending
graduate school at a private college in the state of Illinois.

Reflections

Scholars have constructed a tentative pathway in which undocumented
immigrants make sense of their legal consciousness (Abrego, 2011; Gonzales, 2008, 2011; Gonzales & Chavez, 2012). The first point of awareness happens during the migration process. Individuals either have a
vivid recollection of the discussion, events, and decisions made during
this process or they may not recall any memories associated with their
journey to the U.S. Whether they were active or passive participants

in the migration process, the memories help to inform their legal consciousness. There is much heterogeneity in the migration experiences of these participants that disrupts the nativist master narrative of immigrants, depicting them as reaping the economic benefits of U.S. society. For example, some of the parents highlighted in the profiles had a college degree and were working in professional positions, and many of the participants had documentation upon entry into the U.S. When critically examining these journey-stories, we must acknowledge that the root cause of the violence and economic deterioration of Mexico's rural communities stems from the imbalanced relationship between the U.S. and Mexico. Portes and Rumbaut (2006) maintain that global capitalism is an imbedded hallmark of immigration, which places Westernized (more resourced) countries in positions of power and dominance. The notion of "structural imbalance" (p. 353) suggests that U.S.-bound migration is not individually motivated but historically dictated by the labor demands in both markets (Portes & Rumbaut, 2006). The labor demands in the U.S. warranted a need for workers and crafted recruitment tactics to draw Mexican laborers to the U.S. This gave the U.S. a vantage point as creators of regulations, policies, and practices that determined migration flow.

Trade agreements with the U.S. such as the North American Free Trade Agreement (NAFTA) and the Central American Free Trade Agreement (CAFTA) intensified the migration flow to the U.S. by opening the border to trade capital, goods, services, and information. This, in turn, caused severe economic and social inequities in Mexico and Central America, which are among the reasons the parents of the participants in this study were displaced and decided to immigrate to the U.S. (Abrego, 2011). Rather than placing blame on parents for choosing to immigrate to provide a healthy livelihood for their children, we need to examine critically how U.S. economic and foreign policies are implicating factors within the immigration system.

The social networks among immigrant families demonstrate a sophisticated support structure for undocumented immigrants. The information and knowledge exchange among family members who are considering context and location are informed by the experiences of

immigrants who are already residing in the U.S. This knowledge exchange is an asset and a powerful tool for immigrants transitioning
into U.S. society. I continue to question the kind of impact that family
separation and reunification have on the emotional and social development of immigrant children. Most participants detail how one parent
immigrated prior to the rest of the family. While in most cases both
parents are able to reunite, they also leave behind a family network and
a home country, which they are unable to physically visit. In essence,
family separation and reunification are constant lived factors for undocumented immigrants.

The participants in this study varied in their K–12 experiences,
which were dependent on their local contexts and the availability of
bilingual education programs. As Valverde (2006) indicated, the lack of
efficient bilingual education programs, segregation of immigrant children in the schools, and low academic expectations of immigrant children have a lasting effect. Navigating the linguistic and cultural nuances of the educational system in the U.S. can be a daunting task. There
was variability in the ESL experiences of the participants in this study.
On one hand, some students were able to excel in ESL and be promoted
to "regular" courses. On the other hand, there was also an instinctive
knowledge about ESL instruction that prompted parents and students
to avoid this placement. This is evident when Yahaira's mother fought
against placing her in ESL and Jorge's prior knowledge of ESL; both
experiences exemplify the negative assumptions made by learning in
an ESL environment. Researchers also present the experience of discrimination as a major issue for Latinas/os in their K–12 educational
environments (Bohon, Macpherson, & Atiles, 2005). Schools vary in
resources and support for students with limited English proficiency.
For instance, the lack of certified bilingual instructors or Latina/o instructors adds to the inefficiency of these support programs. Parents
also witness discrimination of their children in schools, which fosters a
culture of mistrust of teachers and schools.

While many of these participants resided in urban locales, some
participants who lived in rural communities were also presented with
a number of new challenges. In a comprehensive immigration report in

rural settings, Jensen (2006) forecasted immigrants increasingly settling in more rural locations rather than urban areas. The findings suggest that rural immigrants are more likely to be Hispanic (and of Mexican origin in particular); they are less well-educated; they are more likely to be poor, but when poor, less likely to receive nutrition assistance; they are more likely to be married; they are more likely to be working, but are also underemployed; they are more likely to own their own home; and they may be in better health and more likely to have access to health insurance.

Yet, the perceptions of this influx of immigrants by community members are mixed. The 20–60–20 rule (Butler-Flora & Maldonado, 2006; Grey & Woodrick, 2005; Jensen, 2006) suggests that 20 percent of the community believe that immigrants are positive contributors to the community infrastructure, 60 percent are indifferent to the impacts of newcomer immigration, and 20 percent have negative perceptions of newcomer immigrants. These negative perceptions often suggest that the increase in immigration is accompanied by higher crime rates. For the individuals in this study, residing in a rural area revolved around the lack of understanding of undocumented immigrant issues on the community's part. In Ariel's case, there seemed to be more empathy and a desire to assist from his community. However, I surmise that these acts of inclusion were more about his academic excellence than they were about his legal status. He was tokenized by his community members to create the illusion of equity without adequately examining the systemic structures that perpetuate discrimination.

Lastly, I was deeply impacted by Alex's testimonial about his notion of higher education. It's presumptuous to assume that colleges and universities are the sole holders of legitimized knowledge and education. For Alex, the community is his school and his direct experiences with organizing and interacting with different institutional agents to fight for queer and immigrant rights cannot be replicated inside a college classroom. Another example of this concept is Yovany's college, Freedom University. These counter-spaces of education and knowledge not only privilege the identities and experiences of undocumented students, but they also offer an opportunity to understand themselves and their legal status identity. This is something that traditional higher education fails to accomplish for undocumented students.

The next chapter focuses on the college experiences of the participants in this study. The two major topics discussed are the strategies used to disclose legal status and the microaggressions that students experience while in college.

Chapter Three

College Access and Experiences in Higher Education for Undocumented Students ... *"Why did they recruit us, if they aren't going to support us?"*

"Incredible," I murmur as I finish reading an email from a concerned community advisor from a youth organization in the Milwaukee area. The email detailed an encounter with a young woman who confided in her that her high school counselor indicated that college was not an option for this student because of her legal status. I roll my eyes and shake my head. "I can't believe that high school counselors are STILL telling undocumented youth that they can't go to college," I state aloud. My mind races and I search for the words to reply to the advisor who searched "undocumented students and the University of Wisconsin Milwaukee," and happened to find my contact information. This counselor profusely apologized for contacting me, and yet I am grateful that she did so. My response email thanked her for writing to me and for taking the step to assist this student as she ponders her college choices. Then in block letters I state, COLLEGE IS AN OPTION FOR UNDOCUMENTED STUDENTS. I had to proclaim this loud and clear. My next email was directed at the Director of Admissions, who I had previously met in a committee meeting. I forwarded this email to him with a lengthy message asking him, How can we be more proactive about educating high schools about working with undocumented students, and what can we do to help this student in her search for opportunities to attend college? The email banter between the Office of Admissions and the counselor was promising. While I felt I had helped one student, I couldn't help but to think about the countless other undocumented students who have been told that college was not an option. It angered me. This is a form of microaggression, but how do we stop it?

There has been a vast amount of studies (Hossler, Braxton, & Coopersmith, 1989; Hossler & Gallaghar, 1987; Hossler, Schmit, & Vesper, 1999; McDonough, 1998) on college choice throughout the years that have examined college choice from a dominant perspective. Recent literature (Chavez, Soriano, & Oliverez, 2007; Drachman, 2006; Flores & Chapa, 2009; Gildersleeve, 2010; P. Pérez, 2010) on undocumented students and college choice and access found that social networks and institutional agents who understand college access from the perspective of undocumented students are key factors. These agents and networks aided in enhancing college knowledge, locating financial aid resources and finding colleges and universities that were in close proximity to their community, families, and home. In an era in which financial aid and scholarship money dictate where students decide to attend college, we must begin questioning whether college is indeed a choice for all. While undocumented students have the option to attend college, their choices are limited by financial constraints, legal status, state policies, and whether undocumented students are privy to the college application process at all. This chapter outlines how undocumented community activists learned about their college options, highlights how their legal status intersected with their ability to navigate college, and depicts students grappling with depression and microaggressions.

College Access and College "Choice"

For the participants in this study, the decision to attend college was not always intentional. While some knew that college was an option they desired, others in the study had no intention of attending because they were unaware of the avenues to college access. One of the barriers to college access was the request on applications for Social Security numbers. Yahaira explains that it leaves students feeling "stuck":

> I was super involved, I was in everything that I could be in because I thought it would help me get to where I wanted to be and go to a great school and do all these wonderful things. And it just kind of hits you that that's not going to be you. Everybody else is talking about all of these things that they're doing and looking at colleges, and filling out applications, and doing all this stuff.

You just stare at applications that ask if you're a citizen or not and you're kind of like, 'Well, shit, I don't know what I'm supposed to do.'

Some of the participants in this study accessed college information through social media. Yovany had been employed at McDonald's for two years after he graduated from high school when he found out about his college possibilities by watching an interview on TV. The television report featured a local undocumented student who Yovany immediately reached out to through social media. The interviewee in turn introduced Yovany to Freedom University. Social media networking among undocumented students is a common practice. Juan also shared that when he first learned about his legal status, he took to the Internet (specifically Dreamact.org) to acquire more information about his college options from peers who shared his legal status while navigating college. Both Yovany and Juan used social media outlets to find more information about the college application process and financial aid resources.

The terms "access" and "choice" readily describe the experiences of traditional first-generation college students who have access to the federal financial aid system. For undocumented college students, the term "restricted access" is a more accurate assessment of their lived realities given that some higher education systems and states have devised policies prohibiting undocumented students from accessing admissions, in-state tuition, and financial assistance. This analysis also questions whether undocumented students even have a "choice" when deliberating where to attend college; or do institutional policies, agents, and financial resources decide for undocumented students? The college choice for undocumented students is confined to colleges and universities that are able and willing to create intentional structures of investment. How undocumented students identify those institutions of higher education as "undocufriendly" is accomplished through social networking, connections with other undocumented students, or through guidance counselors and teachers who have sought to find information and develop knowledge systems. For some, the daunting task of locating undocufriendly institutions and resources in states with limited public information parallels finding a needle in a haystack.

The Role of High School Teachers and Counselors: Gatekeepers of Higher Education

Students in this study expressed that at least one empowerment agent or one teacher who knew about their legal status played an instrumental role in how they were able to navigate the process of finding and going to a college. Not having to endure such a complex and multi-faceted process on their own, students were able to explore options with a mentor or teacher who provided support. Sarai considered her college-going process as an emotional roller coaster: "I remember sitting in the back of the classroom. I put my head down and started to cry because it was the moment that I realized that just the dream of higher education was going to be very hard." She disclosed her legal status to her high school counselor and he helped to research scholarships and colleges that would provide her full scholarships, because her family was unable to provide any financial support toward her college education. The majority of participants expressed gratitude for the college research support given by a teacher or high school counselor. In David's case, he had access to a community mentor through a college preparatory program. David's mentor would serve as a "college translator," gathering information and helping David navigate college administrators. Often first-generation students who have their hearts set on attending college may not know the questions to ask of administrative staff.

For Jessica, Arizona's state policies pertaining to undocumented students dictated the college choice on her behalf. Jessica caught the attention of college recruiters from the College of Business at one of Arizona's state colleges. Her academic profile and leadership skills were ideal for a pre-college program; however, she was unable to access the opportunity. She remembers, "They couldn't recruit me because Proposition 300 was just passed, which doesn't allow undocumented students to receive any type of state aid or receive in-state the tuition. So they couldn't get me into this program. They just couldn't do it. I was the asset that they needed."

The participants in this study sought the help of a teacher or counselor to help with the college-going process and many described themselves as "lucky" to receive guidance from high school counselors. While the end of high school is a celebratory milestone for the average young person, the end of public education for undocumented individuals brings forth feelings of uncertainty. Will their academic excellence in high school translate into college prosperity?

Institutional Agents of Support and Institutionalized Support for Undocumented College Students

For many of the students in this study, finding an institutional agent who is not only knowledgeable in assisting undocumented students but who also is supportive through the college-going process was imperative to their success. In the community college space that Jessica occupies, she was able to use her networking skills to identify a "safe or underground" individual who worked with undocumented students. Jessica mentioned a conversation she had with a teacher who suggested she be careful about revealing her status. I followed up by questioning how it made her feel when the teacher said to be careful and she responded, "More secure because that means that I have to be more careful about the stuff that I was doing [activism] because someone would do something against me." In a way, having an "underground" designated counselor for undocumented students pushes them into the shadows. Conversely, we cannot underestimate the hostile climate for immigrants in states such as Arizona, where having a designated individual can be viewed as a measure of safety. Support for many of the participants in this study also came from multicultural affairs offices in which individuals sharing the same ethnic background as the participants could gather and not feel judged. Faculty who taught courses about immigration or social justice were also instrumental and encouraged students to share their stories. One of David's faculty members showed him support by encouraging him to write his story and publish it in the college newspaper; there, he received positive feedback after revealing his status. Ariel and his professors developed a friendship, as one professor took extra steps to support him:

> He always made it seem a priority to him. He would give me advice; connect me with people who he thinks would be supportive. Some faculty, adminis-trators, they were always very good with me and tell me concrete details like contact names and numbers, not just, oh, I support you or empathize with you—they very much take the extra step to mail me articles or call me up one day and ask me how things were going, help me out. One of my professors, who I felt very comfortable with, gave me a donation before I left. He has a band and he gave me all his earnings from his band because of my status. He was my professor but he was my friend.

Going beyond often-superficial support, and toward concrete ac-tions to support undocumented students in college is the ideal. Many colleges and institutions have employed ally training for student lead-ers, faculty, and staff to better facilitate a more welcoming college en-vironment for undocumented students. At his private graduate school, David explains that whoever makes a request, training can be deliv-ered and an ally agreement sheet is signed. He comments,

> They go over it together and it's a checkoff sheet for allies about what they can do, what they have learned, what could they be more open, more conscious and more aware about, the proper terminology or how the laws and policies impact students.

This is one example of how campuses can begin to discuss issues im-pacting undocumented students on campus. However, many ally training programs operate only when individuals are interested in self-development and are not a strict requirement for all employees. Making training sessions a requirement would be helpful in increas-ing knowledge and awareness across campus. This would help over-come the challenges staff and faculty face in many institutions in which knowing about available resources or how to support undocumented students on behalf of the administration is not the norm. In addition to having on-campus mentors, students who were socially active in the community also developed a network of peer support through these activities (see Chapter Five). Three of the participants in this study were first-year graduate students at private institutions, which leaves open the question, Do factors for college support differ for graduate students?

Navigating Graduate School

For the graduate student participants in this study, it should come as no surprise that all of them are enrolled in graduate programs at private institutions given their flexibility with admissions policies. A recent report on undocumented students in private Jesuit colleges begs institutions to employ best practices for recruiting and retaining undocumented students (Fairfield University, Loyola University Chicago, & Santa Clara University Legal and Social Research Teams, 2013).

Of the three graduate students in this study—David, Ariel, and Angelica—one was attending graduate school at a Jesuit college. Although private schools tend to show more openness to undocumented students, barriers still exist in the graduate school context. I asked each of the graduate students what challenges they have encountered while attending graduate school. Ariel speaks to his graduate school experiences:

> A lot of the stuff, I mean specifically as, I'm sure you know by now that the biggest barrier to continue in graduate school is money, how do you afford all these things. And it's something that you know I've been talking about with several undocumented people over at the University, they accepted us, they provided some funding, but they know the funding they give us is obviously not enough to obtain that. And so how do they expect us to come up with the rest is sort of like a, somewhat deceiving if you could think about it in that sense.

Ariel's sentiments ring true for the graduate students who were recruited based on their desire to explore, research, and practice in the undocumented immigrant community. Even when private colleges celebrate the inclusion of undocumented students, there is still a lack of understanding and intentionality behind the retention efforts for undocumented graduate students, as Angelica discusses:

I know that I approached someone regarding career services, and my colleague and I went up to him on the first day of orientation when he was talking about fellowships and connecting with alumni. And we said, okay, that's great. How does that apply to us, because we're undocumented. And he sort of looked at us and said, 'I'm not sure. I'm going to go to a meeting and then we'll see.' So I talked to him afterwards and I said, 'Okay, so how did the meeting go?' Oh, they basically told me that I'm on my own. And, I think I've asked maybe once again, I'm sure he's incredibly busy, but he doesn't seem interested to do that research. And I find that incredibly disappointing that they haven't figured out how they're supposed to help us, because they're the ones who accepted us. And so, with that comes a responsibility where they need to be just as supportive of us as they are of other students.

Both Ariel and Angelica, who attend the same graduate school, question the investment in and dedication to undocumented student education when their institution demonstrates apathy for the retention of undocumented students. Undocumented graduate students lack access to the federal loan system from which citizen graduate students can withdraw funds to support living expenses, books, and professional development opportunities. When providing research and fellowship stipends to undocumented students, administrators have to consider whether the amount disseminated to undocumented students can sustain them without the assistance of federal loans. Embedded in the data, I also found it evident that access to opportunities such as internships, fellowships, and research grants are often not constructed with undocumented students in mind. The question every administrator directing retention resources should ask is "How can undocumented students access and navigate this opportunity?" Dismissing undocumented students' questions or requests is a concrete indicator that institutions are not inclusive of the needs of undocumented students. Recruiting undocumented students without retention resources is like providing a raft without paddles.

Encounters with Microaggressions

Microaggressions manifest as "subtle insults (verbal, nonverbal, and/or visual) directed at persons of color, often automatically or subconsciously" (Solorzano, Ceja, & Yosso, 2000). In a campus context, these can occur in academic and social spaces as well in the K–12 arena (Kohli & Solorzano, 2012). Instances of microaggressions for undocumented students could perhaps include the use of the term "illegal" or "alien" to describe their status or personhood, asking which country they originate from, or feelings of isolation or invisibility while on campus. While Jaen considers New Mexico an immigrant-friendly state, he explained that much of his college access knowledge was not found in his school. He contends,

> They [high school counselors] never informed me, they never told me, they never said, 'You know what, if you're undocumented you can attend any college as long as you graduate from a high school in New Mexico, you can attend a four-year or a two-year college.' And they never mentioned going to college, I don't know what's wrong with the high school system, that the counselors are ignorant. I don't know if they maybe know, but they don't tell everyone, they only tell the people who they think is going to college. I was never informed about this opportunity.

When one is faced with discrimination, it is a common reflex to find a perfectly logical explanation for racism or claiming ignorance of what resources are available to help undocumented students to excuse one of any wrongdoing. Even when students are equipped with knowledge of their rights and policies, they are once again faced with opposition from those in power. During Jaen's attempt to apply to a local community college, he was essentially denied the ability to apply because he lacked a Social Security number. He details this event and states,

> And one of the interesting things that happened was that I didn't know I was going to be accepted into four-year college but I decided to apply to a community college here in Albuquerque. And when I tried applying, the admissions person told me, you know what, you need to bring your Social Security number. They were denying entrance to me and to undocumented students. And the law here in New Mexico says that you are allowed to go anywhere, regardless of your immigration status and as long as you graduate from a high school in New Mexico with a 2.5 or better. And this person denied me the access to towards getting a two-year college degree or an associate's.

Even when state policies have been implemented, there is no real accountability as to how higher education institutions are employing, training, and tracking their success patterns enforcing these policies. This microaggression blatantly denies students' right to education because they lack a nine-digit number. Essentially, even with "immigrant-friendly" state policies such as those in New Mexico, some educators and administrators fail to change their practices or ideological beliefs on immigration. In many regards, access policies for undocumented students continue to be restrictive.

In states such as Wisconsin and Florida, which do not have in-state tuition policies, navigating the admissions world can be complicated and exhausting. In Jorge's case, he was already a college student in Wisconsin when the incoming state governor rescinded the in-state tuition policies for undocumented students. He explains the stark difference in procedures by commenting,

> Before Walker's [Governor Walker] new budget came and went into effect I had already been qualified to get in-state tuition. You just had to sign a paper and that was it. You had the in-state tuition, right? When Walker took it out of the budget, I had to go through an appeal process and there was a lot more paperwork you had to write about your history. Why are you asking for it [in-state tuition] and what are your future plans and all this other information about where you graduated from and everything.

For Jorge, his short-lived experience with in-state tuition ended with a letter indicating that he would have to pay three times the amount in tuition and would endure additional scrutiny and surveillance about his personhood. Every semester he is asked to declare his existence in front of an appeals board. These microaggressions take away a student's dignity, yet they are a common practice in many higher education institutions.

Juan's first semester in community college was filled with agony because the financial aid office asked him for more documentation concerning his immigration status. After signing an affidavit stating he would make attempts to "regularize" his immigration status, the financial aid office kept pressuring him to produce such documents:

After the first semester they would kind a threaten me—not in a bad way but they would officially tell me you need to present more proof of your immigration status or else we're going to take your scholarship away. I remember getting calls from school and they were like 'we're not really sure if we're going to renew your scholarship.' So, I needed to graduate fast because they're on to me and I was unable to foot the bill for this. So my last semester, spring of 2009, I took like 21 credit hours, while working like full-time, 30–40 hours a week. At that point in time, I finished all my requirements for graduation and then surprisingly the school didn't want to give me my diploma. They said that I have to still prove that my immigration stuff was resolved.

These instances of microaggressions certainly warrant an examination of the unnecessary treatment placed on undocumented students. This practice used by this particular institution communicates a blatant disregard of the challenges and barriers experienced by students without documentation in higher education. In addition, this office of financial aid should be cognizant of the time and resources required by students to "regularize" their immigration status. In most cases, students will not be able to change their immigration status without action from the federal government (i.e., Comprehensive Immigration Reform), and even if undocumented students are working toward receiving permanent residency status or other visa options (U-visas), the process for this venture is extraordinarily lengthy and costly. This process does not align with the timetable of earning a college degree.

The use of the term "illegal" within the college context to describe the immigrant community was a trigger point for most of the participants. Some participants found counselors who would ask, "Are you illegal or undocumented?" They often found themselves educating those counselors on the issue. In Jessica's case, she took the time and had the patience to address this microaggression with individuals by explaining, "I ask where are you coming from, or what is the idea, or the meaning of the things that they're saying, and do you know how it affects other people?" "Immigration" is often highlighted in college classrooms; in those settings, the use of "illegal" is often used synonymously with the term "undocumented." Sarai's political science course dealt with the topic of immigration and because this topic is so personal to her lived realities, she had to consciously decide whether she wanted to disclose her legal status to the class:

> So we always talk about immigration all of the time, you know, immigration, immigration, but something that is always talked about is illegal immigration and I just shudder silently because I don't want to make a big scene, but I'm always very vocal about why we don't necessarily use the term 'illegal,' because no human being is illegal. They are, immigrants are victimized, victims of this broken immigration system, it's not their fault. We can change it, we're actually trying to change it but these polices are still in effect that criminalize, marginalize, and just basically do not allow immigrants to integrate into society because it's very difficult. But I'm always trying to be very conscious of other individuals because they've never met an undocumented student, they've only read it in the books.

For Sarai, being more cognizant about how others will react to her knowledge is what dictates how she proceeds with challenging notions of microaggressions. While most of the participants in this study are comfortable with using a classroom moment to educate those about the hurtful use of the term "illegal," this excuses professors by not being forthright about the use of "illegal" as being interchangeable with "immigrants without documentation."

Living with Depression

There is an initial sense of brokenness when students first begin to intellectualize the impact of their legal status. Some of the research unveils (Ellis & Chen, 2013) how positive actions and reactions to resolving issues around students' legal status allow them to develop their legal status identity in more positive ways. While existing research often posits that "addressing various aspects of being undocumented facilitates opportunities for growth and a sense of personal growth" (p. 260), scholars must also acknowledge the emotional depletion, depression, anger, and healing that continue to occur during this process. For the participants in this study, many contended that their lived experiences as undocumented individuals in U.S. society resulted in feelings of depression due to the restrictive nature of their existence. Yovany described his reality this way:

> I have the privileges of driving and so from there you are limited to the destinations you can go or you're limited in the jobs you can have. The job that you do have is limiting because it's a small income such as McDonald's. You are there working from seven to seven, which I usually do and it's like jail. It's gruesome. You feel like there's no escape and the time you do have you invest in sleeping.

This restricted existence seeps into any type of planning for future prosperity. For these students, the realization of not being able to access a college education, not because of their own design but because of their legal status, led them to spiral into a deep depression. Yahaira has already faced depression a couple of times: when she came out as queer, and when she was trying to figure out how to obtain a college degree with no initial support. As Yahaira puts it, "Then people say, 'Well there's nothing I can do'; so just really feeling really alone, just dealing with a lot of loneliness and a lot of depression that brought about, because not really seeing a way out, not seeing a future." During our conversation, I asked whether she has gotten past her feelings of depression and she responded,

> I mean it was so bad I think at some point I contemplated suicide. Never followed through with it, obviously, but it just gets really, really bad. As far as how I got past it, I don't know if I actually did. I think after that I just felt like I didn't even deserve it. And I, when I went to college I kind of made a lot of stupid decisions because, even though I got into the school, and even though I got a scholarship, it didn't matter because I wasn't going to be able to do anything that I wanted in the end anyway.

An ebb and flow of depression is a constant factor in these participants' lives. Feelings of depression linger and become most apparent when life decisions are to be made or even when milestones are achieved. Juan clarified that his depression was not related to a negative self-image or self-esteem. He explains:

I think my depression is just fueled by anger that I can't do this. I would just have these internal struggles where I would not be okay and completely down on the wire one day and then the next day it's like okay well I need to do this because I need to prove to myself that I can. So it was definitely a give-and-take type of situation. And it still is.

For Juan, anger motivates him to achieve his goals as he continues to live with this form of depression. While all the participants mentioned a "dark phase" in their life, I was particularly struck most by hearing Marco's story as he has attempted to make meaning and intellectualize his own struggles with depression as a college student. The following excerpt is from our conversations about accessing the counseling center on campus:

I guess in retrospect, I definitely should have gone to the counseling center or sought help. I did take a physical test or have a physical done on me prior to going, again, to D.C., just because [the internship site] they required it and kind of hoping that they would have said something or prescribed something then, but physically, I was totally fine. I just remember that, too, that I should have probably been more intentional about searching for help, but at the same time, thinking, 'I don't think the counseling center will know how to deal with an undocumented student.' They probably could have heard me out and it would've been a therapeutic experience. I guess one last point about the counseling center. I wasn't exactly sure, too, if my health insurance with my mom would have covered it, which I think it would not have or I would have gone there, but I just had all those other excuses, too, about access. We definitely did have access just because depression or anxiety was pretty prevalent on campus now. Coming out with being undocumented and talking a little bit about the depression in my narrative and doing some research about the depression in my age group in general, just had more of those conversations with some of my peers. Nothing's overcome. The access issue and the stigma of depression and counseling services are still there.

The belief that therapists or counselors do not have the knowledge or capacity to assist undocumented students grapple with their lived experiences is common. Yahaira was able to access counseling services but she mainly utilized her sessions to explore her ethnicity and queer identities. Juan also accessed mental health services but found his experience to be a waste of time because the therapist at the time was unknowledgeable and unfamiliar with issues facing undocumented immigrants. What I also found interesting in Marco's case was a sense of guilt for experiencing depression:

> I hated being depressed because it was just so self-absorbed and that, I was like a scholarship student who didn't have to pay their way, who didn't have to have one or two jobs on the side to do it, but could actually have the luxury to be depressed. I was very much a very happy college student and fulfilling also what college was offering me but still kind of living with depression about being undocumented. I think just like the time kept on ticking in my head and I think it was very selfish, I mean I think that's why I was just so frustrated with the depression because it was like so centered around my own personal timeline of graduation.... But that totally revolved around me and then I was upset that I was making all of these preoccupations and frustrations still based on my own experiences. I mean I think that's part of the experience of depression, that it's so contained inside your mind and then it just kind of feeds itself. So I mean I think that itself is also frustrating and adds to the weight.

Marco claims that he was great at masking his frustrations and mentions that on the surface he was a happy college student taking advantage of all that college had to offer. Inside he struggled with these frustrations of depression, which, as with hiding his legal status, he was able to mask. When asked about where he is at with his depression and how he continues to cope, he responded:

> I think that's kind of like the challenge where I wrestle with right now is that how to not let it become so depressive and so, again, like self-contained that it just paralyzes me. Because, I think it's frozen a lot of old thinkers about why are we still kind of wrestling with the same basic questions about how to live. I think the only thing that can break that is that there's just so much deep hurt and so much deep need within the undocumented community.

Reflections

The experiences of undocumented students in this chapter highlight the challenges of not only accessing information and the financial resources to attend college, but also navigating all the burdens of their status while attending college. I was most struck by the notion of "luck" that these participants were able to receive guidance from one teacher, counselor, or mentor who provided advice to accessing scholarships and financial support. While these students felt lucky to access these resources, it implies that those who are not able to access college information or resources are "unlucky." It fails to acknowledge institutionalized racism and xenophobia as the culprit of inadequate college preparation support. It is within the job description of all high school counselors to prepare students for post-secondary experiences. These post-secondary experiences are not unique to U.S. citizens and should include the knowledge, training, and resources to support undocumented students.

Institutional agents, such as high school counselors, mentors, and teachers, are crucial in bridging social capital in order for undocumented students to explore various sources of college access (Garcia, 2013). The participants mentioned connecting with other undocumented students on social media to gain information or knowledge about college access and others mentioned faculty members who served in validating roles. When Ariel considers one of his faculty members "as a friend," this exemplifies the meaningful bonds in which institutional agents become empowering agents (Stanton-Salazar, 2011). The empowerment of social capital or empowering agents act in order to disrupt the hierarchical systems to produce "counterstratification" (Stanton-Salazar, 2011, p. 1096). While individual and collective acts from empowering agents are greatly needed in higher education, creating counterstratification systems of higher education would entail the redistribution of resources to individuals most in need.

The microaggressions experienced by undocumented students can be largely attributed to the historical residue of white supremacy (Pérez - Huber, 2009). Essentially, use of the term "illegal" to frame undocumented immigrants obliterates the immigrants' personhood; therefore, they become non-human. In many ways, these dominant perspectives become normative in the public discourse, which negatively positions (un)documented Latina/o immigrants as jeopardizing the existence of U.S. society (Chávez, 2008; Pérez - Huber, 2009). College choice, access, and the persistence of barriers for undocumented Latina/o immigrants are rooted in white supremacy. For Jaen, even though he resides in New Mexico, which has granted in-state tuition to undocumented students for nearly a decade, barriers to college access will continue to exist because racist nativism (Pérez - Huber, 2009, 2010) has yet to be interrogated. Ideological barriers are also evident in the college persistence process. In Juan's case, his institution's threatening to sever his tuition scholarship for not producing immigration forms not only created a hostile climate, but also blatantly dismissed his position as a college student. In many ways, the loss of personhood for undocumented students is perpetuated in the practices of higher education.

Mental health in the undocumented population is another issue that warrants attention. As depression continues to be a constant theme, researchers (Portes & Rumbaut 2006; Suárez-Orozco & Suárez-Orozco, 2001; Sullivan & Rehm, 2005) have unveiled the emotional effects of the migration experience (crossing the border, leaving family behind, and reason for migration) causes stress. For undocumented individuals, the lack of legality limits resources and mobility, which can produce feelings of isolation and fear (Sullivan & Rehm, 2005). The onset of depression is often activated when emotional support is absent. Perhaps the silent stance taken by some institutions of higher education may be interconnected with the depression experienced by undocumented students. By not highlighting available resources, by not creating a system of support in all facets of the educational system, or by not hiring skilled counselors who are specifically trained in this topic further push individuals to feelings of depression. In Marco's case, I empathize with his guilt for feeling depressed. These feelings stem from how current immigration policies and practices have "Othered" (Said, 1994) undocumented immigrants, causing students not to feel entitled to grieve, feel sadness, occupy space, and/or examine the oppression that they have internalized as a result of the immigration system in the U.S.

The urgent question of "Why did they recruit us if they aren't going to support us?" sums up the tension between institutions wanting to be inclusive of undocumented students and undocumented students feeling excluded in college. Often colleges and universities employ silence as a way to internally contain the issue of undocumented students. Using silence as a tactic to "protect" undocumented students may lead to misinformation, lack of procedural practices, and lack of support when colleges and universities do not give voice, space, and resources to undocumented students. Institutions of higher education make undocumented students feel undesired and dismissed when their issues and concerns are afterthoughts; these feelings can lead to attrition. The questions for higher education to grapple with are, How can colleges and universities take a humane stance on supporting undocumented students? Can institutions of higher education truly practice and celebrate equity and diversity if undocumented students are excluded from the conversation due to a lack of institutional support?

Chapter Four

Unpacking the "Staying In" and "Coming Out" Process ... *"Yeah, it's kind of funny because every time I tell someone I don't have papers, they're like, 'No way, are you serious?'"*

The sounds of brass instruments and drumming filled the air, accompanied by chants of "Up, up with education, down, down with deportation." The blustery Chicago cold winds did not dampen the spirits of the individuals at this rally in front of Daley Plaza who were chanting, dancing, and holding signs and art, demonstrating their solidarity. I watched as one student after another took their place at the podium to detail the mental stress of living under the shadows, their parents' hopes, and the desperation of working toward an educational dream that they feared would not be realized. One by one, they recalled pain and fear and, like a serpent sheds its skin, they shed their antiquated philosophies and chose to act, to come out, and to proclaim themselves as undocumented and unafraid. While my body shivered and my cheeks were wind burned, I stood in stillness as my eyes swelled with tears, fully comprehending that I was witnessing a historic moment on U.S. soil.

The disclosure process for undocumented community activists is complex, fluid, and long lasting. There is no right or wrong way to come out as undocumented, but certainly social contexts and lived realities might impact the rationale for disclosing legal status. To better understand how one chooses to disclose one's legal status, I borrow from scholarship on lesbian, gay, and bisexual identity to unpack the coming out phenomena. In the spirit of transparency, I struggled with attempting to make parallels between these two different populations. While both the LGTBQ population and undocumented immigrants share similar risks and consequences for disclosure, each group brings differences in how members came to know their identities. Those who are undocumented individuals usually first learn about their legal status from immediate family members and never have to worry about losing relationships with those family members as a result of their legal status. LGTBQ individuals may risk the loss of a relationship with an immediate family member as a result of their disclosure, which creates differentials within their support networks. However, using the scholarship on the LGB coming out process is a useful tool to frame the disclosure of legal status for undocumented immigrants.

Coming Out Process for Lesbian, Gay, and Bisexual Communities

Before coming out, individuals grapple with their newfound awareness of their sexuality, attempting to seek information about their sexuality while negotiating whom to tell and not to tell (Coleman 1982). The closet symbolically represents the space out of which LGBTQ emerge; either privately or publically they express their sexual identity (LGBQ) or gender identity (T) in a variety of contexts. Within the LGBTQ social context, coming out is an integral part of the sexual and gender identity development process. In 1978, the first openly gay elected public official from the state of California, Harvey Milk, described the coming out process as a source of liberation:

> Every gay person must come out. As difficult as it is, you must tell your immediate family. You must tell your relatives. You must tell your friends if indeed they are your friends. You must tell the people you work with. You must tell the people in the stores you shop in. Once they realize that we are indeed their children, that we are indeed everywhere, every myth, every lie, every innuendo will be destroyed once and for all. And once you do, you will feel so much better. (bstewart 23, 2008)

However, one critic (Butler, 1993a 1993b) of the in/out binary notion of "coming out" argues the disclosure of one's sexual or gender identity does not insulate the person from stigmatization and oppression. In fact, "coming out" further constructs the heteronormative structures of sexuality and gender by framing the closet as the final passage of identity acceptance, when in fact "being out" and "covering up" are simultaneously operationalized and are more appropriate representations of "outness" management. This is not to insinuate that LBGTQ individuals should not heed Harvey Milk's proposition, but coming out does not necessarily always equate to liberation of self from oppression. Research on undocumented student activists frames the "coming out" process as a political act, as strategic, and as a way to resist and fight for recognition and visibility (Corrunker, 2012; Nicholls, 2013; Negron-Gonzales, 2014). Butler (1993a, 1993b) also maintains that political agitation is warranted to resist the normative and colonized images associated with LGBTQ individuals not only to dismantle power dynamics but also to interrogate the multiplicity associated with identities/categorical bins for sexual and gender identities. The act of coming out is a continual process with more "closets" and management of identity. The next question I address concerns what prompts individuals to come out or to stay in and not disclose their sexual identity.

The Decision-Making Process of Coming Out

Orne (2011) highlights contextual reasoning associated with this decision and suggests that coming out or "staying in" reaps both personal and societal benefits. He identifies fear as one determining factor in which individuals hide or lie about their sexual identity. Individuals are positioned either to live their lives openly and honestly or to live a lie. The decision to come out is a complex one that is affected by possible negative reactions. Some of those negative reactions from respondents may include expression of denial, religious talk, inappropriate and embarrassing questions, and aggressive and shaming comments (Manning, 2014). Positive responses can be active listening, affirmation statements, humor, nods of understanding, and verbal and nonverbal expressions of support (Manning, 2014).

The impact of disclosure to self and others is another motivational factor to consider. Explosive knowledge describes the negative consequences that the act of delivering "the news" would have on self and others. These negative consequences may consist of incomprehension, rejection, discrimination, and stigmatization. The act of concealment can be viewed as a coping strategy against negative consequences and emotional stress (Cox, Dewaele, van Houtte, & Vincke, 2011). How people observe and receive the knowledge about their identity also impacts their "biographical construction" (Orne, 2011, p. 693). Simply put, future instances of coming out are based on prior instances of coming out or by learning how their identities are contextualized in various social settings. Orne (2011) contends that " … reasons to come out and 'stay in' … must be considered simultaneously and in conjunction with social context" (p. 699). While disclosure and social context coexist in the decision-making process, Orne cautions scholars that positioning hiding and lying as "bad" and disclosure as "good" reproduces "disclosure imperative" (p. 695). Disclosure is not a goal but rather a navigational journey contextualized by the realities of social context. Disclosure is also interactional and relational. The narratives below illustrate how undocumented community activists grapple with disclosing their legal status to others. I will discuss en(forced) concealment, intellectualization of responses to disclosure, and contextualization of disclosure space, place, power, and critical forms of disclosure.

En(forced) Concealment

Many students gained knowledge about their legal status from their parents or other family members, who often communicate to them that their legal status should never be a discussion point with individuals outside the circle of family and/or family friends. While the parents' main intention was to protect their families and children, for many students it further stigmatized the notion of being undocumented. For many of the participants in this study, not having proper documentation was something that they intuitively knew at a relatively young age. However, none of the participants understood the magnitude of being undocumented until later in life, as Yahaira, a college graduate from Missouri, recounts:

> Yeah, I would say I always knew, I just never really understood what it meant until I was older. Because I was always told that there, I was, that was information I wasn't supposed to share. Because anything could happen, because somebody could come for them, or for me, or take us away, or all that kind of stuff. So I knew, but more than anything it was like a fear type thing, I guess. It was something you weren't supposed to talk about because my parents were afraid.

The messages given to undocumented children by their parents are also informed by harsh discrimination of immigrants in contemporary U.S. society as Jorge, a junior from Wisconsin, stated, "My mom and aunt, they were like 'don't tell anybody about your situation, I don't know what they can do to you' because—you know, there have been cases where people be hating." The "hate" which Jorge speaks of is further validated by the increase of hate crimes against the Latinas/os and the immigrant population as a result of the anti-immigration propaganda (Southern Poverty Law Center, 2008).

An additional layer of the concealment of legal status is in the excuses or exclusions made by the participants to avoid questions, explanations, or conversations surrounding issues of immigration or their legal status. For instance, Ariel's home state of Washington placed him in close proximity to Canada, where many of his friends enjoyed the luxuries of visiting another country. He commented, "How do you tell your friends ... one day, they are like, come on let's go to Canada, let's do this. I would have to make up lies about why I couldn't do it. I felt bad about having to lie to people." Refraining from travel within and outside the U.S. can be considered a "clue" that may identify an individual without legal status. Another form of active concealment is through the conscious decision not to share their status with others because participants had not made sense of the meaning of being undocumented or had the language to discuss their legal status with others. In many cases, participants' first acts of making sense of their legal status occurred in isolation or with limited knowledge, as Juan, a senior from Florida, explains,

> I would never say anything at work. I would never say anything to my peers. When I went to [a four-year college] I often kept quiet about the stuff. So again, I was in my room—I would rather just deal with it on my own, with my computer, because I just felt that first I had to hide it because again I didn't want the university to find out.

Before many of these social activists discovered other undocumented peers, community organizations, or advocates, active concealment was not necessarily by choice but because of internalization of stigma, the realities of deportation, and by the lack of visible support mechanisms. These examples question whether the notions of active concealment are indeed "forced" by the social and political systems, realities, and contexts rather than being a choice.

Intellectualization of Responses to Disclosure

Grappling with the responses to disclosure from others is a continual role for most undocumented individuals. The most common responses are an apparent lack of understanding associated with the ramifications of not having documentation. Jorge had to disclose his status to his high school counselor once he decided to apply to college. He retells, "She didn't even know how to react. She asked, 'You mean undocumented or are you illegal?'" Using "illegal" and "undocumented" synonymously has been highly contested in the media ("Drop the I-Word," 2014). Another example involves disclosure of status to peers. Sarai, a sophomore from California, details an incident in which she disclosed her status to her peers:

> I told one or two friends, but they just didn't really know what to say. It was kind of like, oh, not pity, but sympathy, but they just didn't know how to vocalize it because at that age you just don't know what's going on in terms of politics, you don't know much, right? So I didn't really tell anyone.

In essence, the reactions of the "receiving individuals" are highly dependent on their experiences, knowledge, and realities. Yahaira's experiences of coming out to her high school principal influenced how she proceeded to disclose her legal status later in life. As she notes,

> But I think once I started being in situations where people had to know, it was very humiliating. Humiliating in the sense that people were just very defeatist about it and not like supportive about it.... I was questioned once when I was 16 by a principal, he questioned why I was there. And my question was, 'Why am I here in the country or why am I here in school?' And he said, 'Either one, it doesn't matter.' That was my principal. Like those kind of things definitely set a precedent as to why I was not open with college administrators about my status.

While Yahaira was more open about her status with faculty members, her early "defeatist" experiences kept her more guarded about her status with college administrators. Angelica had a similar experience in which one of her past experiences also influenced how she navigated her legal status in the context of a college internship. She explains,

> I remember that one of my internships I was offered a job and was told, 'There's this position available, would you be interested?' And I had to say that I couldn't, that it was going to be just a conflict with my schedule because I felt I couldn't say to them, 'No, I can't do it because I'm undocumented.' And there were some other opportunities that I know came up for other internships and I was really interested, but I felt very awkward and I guess based on past experience of disclosing my status and saying, this is my situation, this is my challenge and the—with my counselor not really actively helping me and but just sort of saying, 'Okay, well, I'm sorry, I don't know what to tell you' I was reluctant to put myself in that same situation. And so I was limited in that sense of internships.

Angelica's prior experiences with counselors being indifferent to her or unwilling to find resources hindered her ability to put herself in situations (work environments) in which she would have to disclose her status. For many of the participants, disclosure was often met with acceptance among individuals, but each disclosure comes with intentionality and negotiation. Juan recalls a time when he had a mental checklist of questions for himself prior to disclosing his status to others:

And I would just kind of like run my checklist by them—like is this person going to agree with what I have to say even if I reveal my status—yes or no? Is this person sympathetic to my situation? Or will he or she comprehend why I'm doing what I'm doing? And depending on that— whether the pros and cons cancel each other out or outweigh each other I'll say yeah, okay, that's fine.

The navigation of the responses of others adds an additional layer to how the participants decide whether or not to stay hidden or disclose their status. These stories also illustrate the power and control that negative responses may have on future decisions, which may lead to missed opportunities. With each interaction, participants are consciously thinking about the "respondent's" worldview of undocumented immigrants, perhaps in preparation for a conversation about the respondent's reaction, as Angelica concludes,

I'm always trying to be very conscious of other individuals because they've never met an undocumented student; they've only read it in the books. Or not even then, just read about the policy, but they've never put a face to the issue, so I try to be very conscious that oftentimes these individuals don't encounter a lot of immigrant youth.

Contextualization of Disclosure Place, Space, and Power

These narratives center on the influence of context and the role it plays in the participants' decision to disclose their legal status. By understanding the political context of the college climate, the state's political context, and the power of their story, the participants discerned whether or not they would be open about their status to others. For Juan, upon arriving at his four-year college, he understood the political climate of his location to be unwelcoming to undocumented immigrants, as he recounts:

When I went to college, I just kind of swore to myself that I'm eight hours away from home, I'm in a very semi-conservative locale with people who have very harsh opinions as to what immigration is and who have never been exposed to this type of thing so I'm just gonna keep my mouth shut and I'm just gonna pretend that I'm just an advocate—a very interested party.

Juan, although he was open about his status to close peers and an active member of a social activist organization, was viewed on his campus as the "kid who was very obsessed with immigration." He feared that if he disclosed his status to the university administration then "they could take action on me and then retroactively take away my tuition money and then foot me a bill for the amount that I was incorrectly charged." On top of navigating the typical burdens of college life, Juan had the additional task of navigating the political context of his campus for undocumented students.

The classroom served as a space in which participants often question how much of themselves they wanted to disclose. For most, some courses offered opportunities for discourse around the topic of immigration. Jorge, a civil engineering major, mentioned that his classes were not conducive spaces in which to disclose his legal status. He states, "Most engineering students are very apolitical. They mostly concentrate on their studies and the ones who are politically conscious are pretty conservative. So I don't talk much about my status…. I'm not very open about it in the classroom because I know they won't understand." For others, the topic of immigration was too personal or too close to home to participate in. Silence was used to deflect the attention from themselves. Juan, a political science major, perhaps felt it was too challenging to participate in heated immigration conversations while trying to maintain his composure. He recalls,

There were literally times where I really wanted to rip like people's heads off and just be like your argument is invalid by so many points. But for the sake of keeping a civilized and nurturing academic environment I will just shut up. I think there was this individual—we had like a class debate in my sophomore year, like it was like Government 101 or something like that and … the elections were coming around and we had a small debate and this person started talking about how immigrants don't pay taxes or whatever the case may be and I think I really did step out of the lines in that one instance but outside of that no, outside of that I just kind of kept my composure and always very respectfully always asked if someone else was going through this, not myself.

On the one hand, for Juan "stepping outside the lines" equates to confronting immigration myths with a heightened sense of passion and anger, which is normal given the nature of the topic, but taking a neutral stance and maintaining silence as a coping strategy to hide his legal status. On the other hand, Angelica, who is attending graduate courses at a private college, has disclosed her status in the classroom setting before but cautiously considers many factors before deciding to disclose. She explains,

> I think if I'm trying to make a point or if I want someone to understand something, then I'm more willing to share my experience. Or people who understand civic engagement, or are interested in activism. But when I see someone that's just sort of asking just to sort of know or just because, and I think it depends on the intention that I'm sort of interpreting. And, in that particular case, it just seemed so much more superficial, where we were all going around and saying where we were from, the university that we had attended, when we had graduated, what our degree was in. And so it just seemed very superficial and I guess I have a lot of respect for my story.

Angelica uses her intuition to assist in deciding, and names the class activity or environment as "superficial," which created a space in which she was uncomfortable telling her story. The respect that Angelica had for her experiences demonstrates not only an awareness of its power but also an understanding of the intention behind its purpose that is something that guides her decision.

Disclosure in the workplace poses a more complex negotiation for some of the participants. While Yahaira considers herself open about her legal status, she finds herself making concessions about disclosure because it might impact her livelihood. She articulates,

> For example, just last night I was asked [by someone at work], 'You're going to vote, right? I mean because I know you're moving, but you're going to vote.' And even though I'm very open [about status], this is through my business and I do some interpreting at courts, so at these courts people don't know that I'm undocumented. And I mean I'm not fond of it, but I have to pay the bills somehow, and so kind of finding myself in this situation of, I don't know how to answer this question.

This example depicts the contextual situations in which participants are placed in a "revolving door" mode of disclosure. In other words, individuals may simultaneously be out and concealed, depending on the risks that may be involved. This mode is highly contested for some as they are reminded once again that "undocumented and unafraid" is applicable only to spaces and places in which participants intuitively feel the risk of disclosure.

Critical Forms of Disclosure

Like much of the historical coming out platforms, coming out of the shadows is an act of expressing one's human rights as well as putting a human face on the politics of immigration in an attempt to change public discourse. Marco recalls the first few times of coming out as "therapeutic sources." Other participants continue to learn and grow from each coming out experience. Many students used words such as "liberation," "freedom," "a prideful point," and "empowering" to describe the moment in which they could truly be their whole selves. For some, "coming out" of the shadows becomes less about the public forum kind of disclosure or the political action and more about how one can incorporate self in everyday lived experiences. Yahaira describes how she thinks differently about her coming out process:

> To some people, I also feel like coming out is like a very like planned, very methodical type of thing. We have a whole month about it and people get [out their] megaphone and they do this whole shebang for a particular purpose. I'm like, yeah, that's great. But then, my comings out are just like, I crack a joke about it, right? You know, like something comes up and then I'm like in the woes of being undocumented.

In essence, acts of disclosure become part of common conversation that includes humor as a way to incorporate self in everyday lived experiences. Other students try to push for more conversation about legal status and undocumented students when issues of social justice arise. Angelica finds herself feeling frustrated that issues pertaining to a salient part of her identity are often excluded from the conversations within classroom discourse and having to correct instructors about language usage for undocumented individuals, as she notes,

> My first quarter we had a class and our professor kept using the words 'undocumented' and 'illegal' interchangeably, and it got to the point where I was just so irritated that I said, 'They're not interchangeable.' And someone asked why. And it was funny that some people were sort of, were disturbed because obviously they knew the difference and, from the two people who approached me afterwards, they were very happy that I'd spoken up, no one had said anything. And obviously it just shows the disconnect that some, some of my classmates are just now aware, they're not informed, they don't know. So I, I mean it was nice. It was nice to be able to share that and to say, no, it doesn't mean this because the reason, or it means that because of. So I think it's an opportunity to sort of educate and make use of what I can offer.

Angelica assumes the role of the educator in the course and uses her knowledge and prior experiences to dispel myths and combat microaggressions within the classroom. Interestingly, while her classmates agreed with the critiques she unveils, Angelica bears the responsibility of defending the value of bringing forth knowledge pertaining to immigrants.

Ariel and other participants mentioned the thoughtfulness of "framing" self to others when deciding to disclose to others, particularly those in positions of power. For Ariel, additional critical thinking is required when disclosing legal status to a trustee who has the potential to influence policy changes. He contends,

> Coming out outside of the university, outside of the classroom, talking to administrators and working, going to different departments, it becomes a little more complicated. I have to, it's not that I can't be myself, but I have to frame myself in a way that is strategic. I can't just come in and be like, hey, I, my name's [participant name], I'm undocumented, I would in the classroom, I have to think about it twice. When I'm talking to a trustee, for example, about how I can frame myself in a way that I can try to convince that person to utilize not only my experience but also the framing of it in a way that I possibly can get any positive outcomes in that sense. So, and in the classroom, I feel like I can be myself; outside of the classroom, not so much, or at least, at least not as, not as much as I would be classroom.

In a sense, critical disclosure is part of social activism as participants attempt show their whole selves in everyday conversations, inside the classroom, and with individuals who have influence and power to change institutional policy and discourse.

Reflections

By putting a human face on the lived realities of being undocumented in the U.S., one has the power to change the public discourse of immigration rights. There is a sense of liberation, a taste of freedom, a moment of lightness when these community activists disclose their legal status, all intertwined with sparks of anxiousness and relief. As a method of protection, which comes from a place of love and care, families condition their children not to disclose their status. While parents and families instilled a sense of fear about the ramifications of disclosing one's legal status, the blame should not be placed on families, but instead on the system that gives them reason to fear disclosure. This is an example of what Orne (2011) terms the biographical construction of disclosure. These narratives also parallel much of the literature on disclosure, in particular how social contexts (Orne, 2011) play an influential role in how and when participants decide to disclose. Orne's notion of coming out and "staying in" was also apparent in this study. For instance, Yahaira's concealment of her status in her professional capacity signifies a high level of awareness of organizational climate, which does not negate the pride she feels about her legal status. Rather, she is strategic and understands the ramifications that her status has on sustaining her livelihood. The underpinning rationale behind Yahaira's decision is based substantially on the lack of employment opportunities for undocumented immigrants. There is no structural or institutionalized "protection" or policy for undocumented individuals in a workplace environment, which poses a different sociopolitical context and reality than those who have a disability or who want to express their sexual orientation, ethnic/racial identity, or religious beliefs.

Rationale for concealment coincides with the literature (Dalgin & Gilbride, 2003; Poindexter & Shippy, 2010; Patton, 2011; Ragins, Sing,

& Cornwell, 2007) in terms of negative repercussions from others, fear of judgment, and stigma resistance. However, the way in which people learn about their hidden identity or how the internalization of stigma impacts future disclosure decisions is unveiled in this study. The act of hiding or concealment was ingrained within the socialization process for the participants in this study. The current immigration structures and system reproduce invisibility or an "underground" existence because of the harsh anti-immigrant sentiments and the fear of deportation. The further analysis of the en(forced) concealment finding speaks to the responsiveness to the inequities existing within the immigration system. Parental or family knowledge and experiences inform how knowledge is disseminated to children with the intention of protecting them from an anti-immigration society; there are no institutionalized modes of "protection" for undocumented immigrants; therefore, we cannot fault parents for the reproduction of stigma within their family unit.

While the fear of negative responses and judgment precludes individuals from disclosure, the narratives also demonstrated that dehumanizing comments toward the individual and lack of assistance (inaction) in finding resources contributed to how one proceeds to disclose in future events. Angelica's example about not disclosing her legal status when she was offered an internship opportunity was informed by a prior instance in which a counselor assumed a defeatist approach to her status ("Okay, I don't know what to tell you"). This is not to say that students cease disclosure of legal status, but these defeatist responses add to their reluctance in future disclosure. In Angelica's case, she perhaps missed an internship opportunity that could have aided in her future endeavors. Another critical examination of the findings suggest that negative responses from others could be informed by anti-immigration propaganda and their defeatist responses may be based on ideological beliefs as well as lack of knowledge on this issue.

Context was another influential consideration for participants to disclose their legal status. In some cases, an understanding of campus climate, locale of the university, and state politics comes into the forefront as factors affecting disclosure. More specifically, participants were less inclined to discuss topics of immigration in the classroom setting because of personal connection to the topic or other classmates perceived as being not knowledgeable on the topic. Certainly the difference between the undergraduate and graduate classroom climate may play a role in how knowledge about immigration is facilitated and constructed. Yet, the example of a professor using the terms "illegal" and "undocumented" synonymously in the classroom context does speak to the lack of critical examination of immigration issues on the professor's part. An important component of these findings is that the existence of undocumented individuals in common spaces such as college classrooms or in one's daily interactions is perceived as an afterthought. Legal status is more often not included in discussion of social justice in such issues as race, class, and gender. The apparent lack of information or discussion about citizenship privilege reproduces notions of dominance within segments of immigrant population.

The ways in which the participants regard their story or their legal status as a means to educate or persuade others was evident. This element addresses the purpose and impact of telling their story. Central to some of the decisions to disclose were gauging positive responsiveness and the ability to change the opinions of others. For some, depending on the level of power of an individual, participants thought about "framing self," perhaps in more palatable ways in order to gain the attention of those who may have limited knowledge or contact with undocumented immigration issues and people. In other words, participants are also concerned about the actual presentation of their legal status disclosure and approach potential situations with intentionality and purpose. Perhaps this is a form of "strategic management" in which the participants deflect the multifaceted "controlling images" (Hill Collins, 1999) of undocumented immigrants, which may be adopted as the dominant discourse, truths, or master narratives.

Chapter Five

Social Activism and Defining "Undocumented and Unafraid"

... "After years of feeling powerless, feeling ashamed, and feeling afraid and to see people who have that courage and conviction to do something"

Reflections from the Milwaukee YA BASTA rally: Babies. Two girl siblings clasping each other as they muster up the courage to speak into the microphone. The little one is 9 and the older one is 13. The older wipes her tears away and relaxes her shoulders, exhales all her fears out as she prepares to speak to a crowd of 100 people standing in front of her. The four o'clock sun beams in her eyes as she squints for relief. She speaks with compassion as she details how her father was preparing to drop them off at school when the police officer stopped him on his way out of the garage. She said, "I knew what was about to happen but I had to be strong for my little siblings who were still in the car waiting for him." The police detained him and he was processed for deportation. These babies were pleading for their father to come back, a father who, according to his daughters, "always taught us to be proud of who we are, to not be ashamed of where we come from, and supported our studies and our mother." This day allowed each family, one by one, to give voice to the impact, the emotional blow, and the chaos that caused these families to feel so much pain at the hands of ICE. The questions from the audience: "Why is Obama backstabbing the community that got him elected? Why?" I felt droplets of sweat roll down my back as I unleashed the tears that were welling up in my eyes. In my heart, I hurt for these children and their families. The trauma that deportations have caused the immigrant communities is irreversible. To whom can we entrust the lives of our family members if promises have been broken, and politics and votes come before people? I close my eyes and plead with the universe to make one of these children a future president or politician. It will take those who have suffered pain at the hands of our government to make the changes we need to see in our communities.

For the past five years, it seems as though not a week goes by without a petition for the release of an undocumented detainee, who perhaps was picked up by ICE while driving, showing up to his/ her job, or simply being in the wrong place at the wrong time. Social activism and community organizing never sleep for undocumented immigrants. This is one reason the work, the experiences, and knowledge of the community activists in this book are so imperative in the fight for human equity. The previous chapter revealed the many reasons, contexts, and forms of how participants in this study disclose their legal status. In this chapter I make historical parallels between the immigrant youth movement and the Chicana/o movement of the 1960s by discussing five theoretical explanations of social activism. I then examine how individuals define the notion of "undocumented and unafraid," the fluidity of fears, and the lessons of social activism. Finally, I introduce the term "critical legal consciousness," which illustrates how some students have cultivated a more nuanced and critical viewpoint of the U.S. immigration system through social activism in the form of resistance, thus (re)constructing their own legal identity.

Chicana/o Movement and the Undocumented Youth Movement

I remember sitting in my first U.S. Latina/o Studies course when I began to realize how little I knew about my ethnic background. Rodolfo "Corky" Gonzalez, Dolores Huerta, and Caesar Chavez were names that I should have learned in my formative schooling but it was during my collegiate years that I gained access to my history, including the Chicana/o civil rights movement. Part of me felt validated and powerful, while the other part of me was angered that my U.S. history courses in high school and college blatantly omitted the contributions of Mexican Americans from my learning. Not only did my new knowledge about my history and culture provide me with self-awareness, confidence, and pride in my ethnic identity, it also gave me the tools to intellectualize my college surroundings. The 1960s Chicana/o student movement's quest to diversify college campuses allowed me to make parallels to contemporary struggles with educational inequities for Latinas/os in the U.S.

In 1969, the first National Chicano Youth Liberation Conference was held in Denver, Colorado, to set the stage for the national agenda for civil rights, nationalist ideology, and defining Chicana/o self-identity. Chicana/o college students began to understand the purpose of taking a revolutionary stance by making their college education beneficial to the overall community, rather than using education as a stepping-stone to increased individual socioeconomic mobility—an accepted core value of American society (Muñoz, 1989). As a result, this prompted Chicanas and Chicanos to enter college with nationalist and revolutionary attitudes, which ignited Chicana/o student activism on college campuses. Approximately one month after the National Chicano Youth Liberation, a group called the Chicano Coordinating Council on Higher Education (CCHE) held a conference at the University of California at Santa Barbara to discuss how the community and the students could work together to increase educational access. In attendance were hundreds of student leaders, community activists, and graduate students. They published *El Plan de Santa Barbara* (Muñoz, 1989) that sent a strong message to universities:

> Chicanismo draws its faith and strength from two main sources: from the just struggle of our people and from an objective analysis of our community's strategic needs. We recognize that without a strategic use of education, an education that places value on what we value, we will not realize our destiny. Chicanos recognize the central importance of institutions of higher learning to modern progress, in this case, to the development of our community. But we go further: we believe that higher education must contribute to the information of a complete person who truly values life and freedom.

The destiny of our people will be fulfilled. To that end, we pledge our efforts and take as our credo what Jose Vasconcelos once said at a time of crisis and hope: 'At this moment we do not come to work for the university, but to demand that the university work for our people.' (Muñoz, 1989, p. 192)

In an attempt to make the connection between the Chicana/o movement and the contemporary undocumented immigrant youth movement, I use and briefly describe five theoretical explanations for social activism (Gómez-Quinones & Vásquez, 2014) to situate the social activism engagement of the participants in this study. The first is generational theory, which positions youthful individuals (under 35) to be more likely to have unmet needs, experience psychological setbacks, and harbor resentment toward individuals who have power. In any social movement, one finds older adults advocating along with youth activists; however, historically, youth have been the key drivers of social movements. Generally speaking, the youth activists are conveyed as the popular image within the immigration movement. For example, more than 500 undocumented students arrived in Washington, D.C., during the summer of 2009 for the "Back to School Day of Action" in order to garner support for the DREAM Act, and in January 2010, four students walked 1,500 miles from Miami, Florida, to Washington, D.C., to generate awareness and support for immigrant issues in the U.S., appropriately named the "Trail of Dreams." Within the last decade, young people have controlled most of the immigrant rights movement.

The second is breaking down/reconstitution theory, which explains how old ideologies, policies, and practices are ill equipped to address new social conditions in society. Basically, this paradigm examines how perhaps maintaining the status quo reproduces systemic inequities. For instance, in-state tuition policies that have been passed in 17 states can be viewed as an attempt to provide "financial relief" to undocumented students. The resurrection of DREAM student centers on college campuses is also a step in bringing visibility and college support to students without documentation. Lastly, Deferred Action for Childhood Arrivals (DACA), President Barack Obama's executive order, provides some undocumented individuals with the opportunity to work legally in the U.S. These examples depict a few policy implementations that strive to provide undocumented students with support and resources; however, none of these policies addresses legitimate pathways toward citizenship. The attempts to bring relief to undocumented immigrants is somewhat masked in conventional thinking, because an expedited pathway to citizenship is the first step to dignified equity for this population.

It is via the social movement/resource model that groups and individuals articulate the means by which they hope to gain resources. In this position, activists have to strike a balance between the priorities of those on the front lines and those who are advocating from the sidelines. This explanation also gives credence to the notion that one unified movement is nonexistent. An example of this model is in the differing strategies and purposes of United We Dream (UWD) and the National Immigrant Youth Alliance (NIYA). While dominant in the immigrant youth movement, both groups strive to enhance awareness and create policies inclusive of undocumented families and communities. Although their missions are parallel, the tactics and strategies used to carry out their mission have political and ideological differences. For instance, UWD works closely with political operatives and partners with a number of advocacy groups across the nation. NIYA's mission and core values acknowledge that political advocacy alone is not enough and it employs intentional forms of civil disobedience to heighten awareness, provide education, and empower its community. Both organizations are valuable to the immigrant youth movement but they highlight how resolutions, conversations, and negotiations vary among immigrant youth ideologies and purposes.

The last two paradigms for social activism are the most relevant to this research project. Change and motivational factors focus primarily on the self, and trying to change the attitudes and opinions of others through activist work. At the same time, activists develop themselves, formulate new ways of thinking and feeling, and critically reflect on themselves and the society that they are attempting to change. Gómez-Quinones and Vásquez state, "Human psyches under assault multiply in an authoritarian, patriarchal, racist, homophobic, and avaricious society" (2014, p. 11). Activists reclaim dignity and freedom through fighting for equity in a holistic sense. Equally related to the fourth explanation is how intersecting identities of gender and sexuality play a pivotal role in activism, as dominance and patriarchy can seep through the social movement and create an oxymoronic climate by perpetuating oppression in an equity-driven movement. These theories provide foundational substance for the following sections. What these community activists add is an intentional mention of family (parents specifically) as part of the reason they engage in social activism. The homage they pay to their families can serve as an additional explanation for social activism (which I discuss in this chapter).

Why Social Activism?

During my conversations with the participants in this study, I asked them why they "do" social activism, what propelled them to be part of this large community-organizing mechanism. Their responses varied; for some, the activism work began as an educational tool and as a way to gain more knowledge. Others had previously identified as community activists and already were advocates concerning other issues. For example, Alex was already passionately coordinating and leading efforts in the LGBT movement through his nonprofit work educating Latino gay males on HIV issues. He became aware of the undocumented immigrant movement through public demonstrations that were held in Los Angeles. He recalls,

> The first time I heard about the DREAM activist movement [was] after I graduated high school during the big marches in 2006. I remember we were going to head out with my friends to go and participate, but I was too scared. I was just afraid of LA. I heard that immigration was heavy over there, even though their reality was mine as well. But in 2010, was the very first time that I was exposed to DREAMer students, putting their lives at the forefront, protesting that they were undocumented and were unafraid. This was one of the first coming out of the shadows events at the UCLA march. I was there. I was with some of my clients [from his nonprofit agency]. You know, that they just invited me and it's funny how it worked differently because I had some of my clients mentoring me about being undocumented and unafraid. And I thought that the support system that we built in the center was amazing,

because we realized we had so many closets and we had a lot of colonization in our minds that we needed to get rid of and how do we get rid of them? We can't just pretend we know it all or that we can empower ourselves, without listening to other experiences, in order to empower us as well.

"Empowerment" was a common word used to describe the impacts of social activism. Oftentimes, the choice to participate in social activism is more personal and hits closer to home, and not necessarily by choice but out of necessity. Angelica recounts her brother's deportation case as a critical event in her life, which she considers transformative. She states,

October 11th of 2010 when my brother was stopped for driving with his high beams on. Even though the officer could have given him a ticket or a warning he decided to take him downtown and so he was processed and they learned of his status. And so he was held by the police and he was in jail for three days. And my family was told that we either pay an immigration bond—a $5,000 immigration bond—or he was going to be sent to Stewart Detention Center in Georgia. We're fortunate that my family was able to pay for the bond but once again there was another battle to come—when we consulted attorneys to see what his options were and to learn that there were no options. And he [attorney] told us that this was the only option and it did not matter that my brother came into the country when he was 3 years old. He was a student, no prior criminal record ... and so my brother was going to take voluntary departure and was going to go as well. Because I was absolutely disappointed and frustrated, to realize how we're being treated, to see him criminalized, not being able to continue my education.

This incident caused local activists and community organizers to rally support behind and awareness of Angelica's brother's deportation case. This is the point at which Angelica realized the power of organizing and using civil disobedience as an educational tool. Among other reasons, motivating others to pursue higher education or to seek support from the undocumented community were factors for participating in social activism. As David states,

I know there are other folks behind me who are thinking about going to school and being able to act as a role model really motivates me and letting them know that they are capable of reaching their goals and going to college and being much more. It also takes patience and it takes hard work. I don't think it's hindered me in any way really. It's been the opposite. It's fueled me even more. Also, I don't know, it's a self- empowering feeling of knowing that you are taking initiative to start a conversation, to do workshops—in particular, knowing that you are educating others about a topic they are passionate about.

David in particular talked about being patient with himself and others when participating in social activism. For many, social activism is defined by the actions that undocumented individuals take in order to bring consciousness, resources, and resolution to change policies that exclude this segment of the population from fully participating in U.S. society. Beyond the action, participants gain skills, cultivate personal growth, and create a strong network of allies. Missing from these social activist narratives is a self-centeredness; rather, there is a focus on the collective needs of immigrants. Their work is centered on the larger topic of immigration and social justice rather than fighting for individual benefits for themselves. The sacrifices made by their parents, who endured harsh living realities, were also main reasons for taking action, sometimes seen as paying homage to them. Ariel keeps the memory of his father as motivation to continue his activist work. He retells a time in which his father was able to join him in an immigration rally:

I'm from a town of about 47,000 extremely Republican, wheat fields all around, and agriculture is your number one income. But in the downtown streets of a small town, every time I remember it makes me just a bit emotional in that sense. I was walking and this reporter from the local paper, conservative paper, interviewed me, and they asked, 'Why are you doing this, why are you here, why are you not in class?' And I said, 'For my father, he's here with me. And he deserves an opportunity just like I do.' And my dad was right there with me waving both his Mexican flag and American flag. And to me I guess that sort of stuck in my mentality of, why I do what I do, because it's not fair because it's unjust and because our parents deserve better. But every time somebody asks me, why do you do the, what you do, and I say, 'Well, I wasn't able to make it to my father's funeral because I couldn't go back to where he was, I couldn't go to Mexico and come back, so, I mean, I was not there for him, I feel he was there for me and I feel like that's an injustice. I don't think that people should not be allowed to go back and see their parent's funeral because of a nine-digit number.

Families are central to activists' work, then, as recognition of the injustices that their undocumented parents must bear, parents who, for the most part, continue to live in fear. The acknowledgment of family separation has taken a mental toll on individuals who cannot return to their country of origin in order to care for ailing relatives, attend family celebrations, or pay their last respects to dying family members. The individuals in this study expressed that while they don't fear deportation for themselves, they most certainly fear deportation of their parents or other family members. Social activism is a tremendous family resource that cultivates social networks and knowledge that can be brought back into the household. Community organizing can also be a healing element.

The Powers of Community Organizing

Stopping deportations, infiltrating detention centers, and participating in sit-ins or other acts of civil disobedience have allowed these social activists to place their trust in their fellow community activists who strategize for the release of detainees. In some cases, participants are able to talk to other undocumented immigrant detainees while in the detention centers in order to make their stories public. Witnessing these powerful exchanges is not only empowering but is also used as a way to understand the removal process. After watching undocumented immigrants released, Angelica started to feel differently about herself:

> I didn't realize the power, the impact of community organizing. I didn't think it was possible to stop deportation. I didn't know that that was a possibility and to realize that it is, that it hasn't happened once and it hasn't happened twice, but it's happened probably hundreds of times. Even right now with the activists that are in Broward Detention Center, it's thanks to them that about 25 people have been released. To see that power that we have, that for me, it's very encouraging to see that after years of feeling powerless, feeling ashamed, and feeling afraid and to see people who have that courage and that belief and that conviction that they can do something and that they will do something.

While not all individuals in this study have participated in sit-ins or experienced detainment in deportation centers, those who have are able to speak to other detainees to learn about the injustices inside these immigration detention centers and how to fight for their removal. Alex highlights this example during his experience in a detention center:

There was a gentleman who was in his 40s and he didn't speak any English and he was undocumented. He had an ICE hold, and he was just like, 'No, I'm going to be deported,' and we had access to a phone, a land line, so right away we were organizing within the detention center facility. And we got all his information and we communicated with authorities and lawyers within the community and we got the ICE hold off him and he was released shortly.

While Alex stated he was nervous about going to jail, he knew the community was going to fight for his release. This is also an example of the magnitude of faith one places on organizers. Marco also speaks of his faith and the trust he places in the community-organizing process.

I'm not careful anymore about going to jail, or being in a deportation proceeding because I trust the organizing that's behind us and I trust the work that we're doing. And going to immigration detention and putting myself in legal proceedings it's, again, validating the work and the thought that I had that I don't think I, again, at the root of it did anything wrong and I'm ready just for the consequences of it. Yeah, I guess I'm still learning, is that how powerful civil disobedience is and how it inverts so many of the tables and how it really challenges power dynamics… . It's so necessary, because people that are underrepresented and seemingly have so little agency, can still challenge the system and still kind of dramatize what injustices they suffer and call attention to it by civil disobedience. Which is why I think it's such a complicated process and it requires so much effort, and time, and energy, because it's not like an easy thing to do. But I think it's also such an important thing to do, and the more people do, it the more people are comfortable with it. And I think within our own community, the more the stigma against it is washed away, the more powerful it becomes, and hopefully the more inclusive it can become of people that aren't coming from, even within the undocumented community, such low-privilege positions.

Participating in civil disobedience is not an arbitrary decision. The individuals in this study talk about "being ready," and joining training camps sponsored by undocumented immigrant organizations in order to understand strategies required to address maltreatment inside the detention center. Some individuals describe the detention center as "cold" in every sense of word. Detention officers try to garner responses from detainees by taunting them to speak, as detainees stay silent waiting for legal representation. Angelica recalls her experiences in detention facilities:

> It is difficult when you're made fun of by police officers and you do feel dehumanized and discriminated and you're cut off from your family and the outside world, in a sense. You're being treated as a child. You don't have any say, it almost feels like, because you're told when to sleep, what to do. To think about people who have put themselves in that situation for a week and to see it as an opportunity to help others; that instead of thinking, 'Oh, I'm in a situation,' they know that others have been there for longer. They don't have those privileges. They don't have those opportunities of having those connections, of knowing, 'No, it's okay. We're going to get out. Things are going to be getting better.'

For most, the purpose of civil disobedience is to be inside the detention centers in order to listen to the stories of other detainees who detail their experiences, their frustrations, and who have been emotionally scarred by the separation from family. But through these acts and by obtaining knowledge, the participants in this study were able to empower themselves. However, Angelica and others bring up an interesting point about the issue of privilege, which questions whether undocumented social activists have privilege. These acts are often highly publicized by the media. Does this privilege these activists because a national audience watches these public acts of civil disobedience?

Acknowledging Privileges

Marco simply puts it, "To talk about a privileged undocumented immigrant that's so, I mean it's almost like an oxymoron." In many ways, living in a society without having a legal presence does not allow one to move very freely and willingly within that society. However, the individuals in this study view their access to higher education and the accumulation of social networks through their activist work as capital.

The privilege that I speak of in this section is not focused on privilege of social identities (this is highlighted in the next chapter), but rather the involvement with a social movement.

Marco pinpoints his ability to intellectualize that being undocumented and unafraid can be posed as a privilege. He explains:

> I'm still in a privileged position to even be thinking about what it means to be undocumented and unafraid and whereas like my folks, my parents own a restaurant and have to work 80 to 90 hours a week. So they have to use their muscles to work so much that their brains are too exhausted to even —I mean obviously they're not exhausted to think because they're very intelligent human beings but to have these philosophical discussions is not really a luxury that they can afford because they have to provide for themselves and have many a times provided for me and for my sister.

The process of making meaning of identities, and the ability to access resources and people who serve as co-contemplators in this process, is considered a privileged space along with many of the students who were able to access financial resources. Not all students were "scholarship DREAMers," and many had to "stop out" of college to find work in order to finance their education. There is a clear difference between those students with a full scholarship and minimal college expenses, and those who had financial support but also worked to live, to pay for school, or to support their families. Even on a college campus, Sarai referred to her experience as "living in a bubble." She had access to resources and people while attending her private elite college and has shifted her focus by advocating for other immigrants who don't have access to college. She elaborates:

> Right now we're at a stage of very, I'm very privileged, I have a lot of resources on campus, I know a lot of people. And also I'm young, I'm educated, I'm a woman. So kind of use those things to your advantage and also use your privileges in terms of being young, being and using to advantage you, to work for a greater good for others that don't necessarily qualify under that. But we have to remember our parents. So we just started reinventing the movement in a way because we're not only focusing ourselves but also including those who are not necessarily, you could say, the perfect 'DREAMer.'

The privilege of being in a college environment, where training to think critically about societal issues begins, does present itself as a luxury in comparison to those undocumented immigrants who are not able to access higher education. The fact that many of the individuals in this study regarded their education as a privilege demonstrates not only a critical self-consciousness, but also an inclination to change the dominant narrative and challenge which immigrants are deserving of opportunities and which immigrants are positioned as not deserving. Do all undocumented immigrants have to be "perfect DREAMers"?

Problematizing the Perfect DREAMer Narrative and the DREAM Act

The abbreviation of the Development, Relief, and Education to Alien Minors (DREAM) Act became the label placed on undocumented students who had aspirations to attend college. A popular narrative has dominated the image of DREAMers: they are those who are high-achieving students, who graduate at the top of their class, who garner accolades in leadership and service within their community, and who society deems as being most "deserving," or as "wasted talent" because they were unable to continue their educational pursuits. The notion of the "perfect DREAMer" perpetuates the assumption that only those with high scholastic abilities or those who most resemble assimilationist perspectives of "American" values are most deserving of legal status. Sarai talks about how she has resources for herself at her private elite college in terms of mental wellness and financial support. Her activism focus has been outside the walls of academia:

> I've been more focusing on, in terms of just bringing all these resources outside of campuses, because that's where you need all the resources, because, sadly, the movement is refocused, I mean mainstream media has mostly been focusing on the image of the perfect DREAMer. You know, UCLA graduate, wants to be a doctor, wants to be an engineer. Yeah, I mean somehow, some way you'll find a way, you'll just find it. But, in terms of those youth that kind of fall through the cracks, those youth don't necessarily have a 4.0, they

haven't been able to go into higher education because they can't afford it, they have to support their parents, or they have to support themselves. So a lot of the resources should be more focused on those youth, and that's what I really focus on, just remembering that the movement is not about the perfect DREAMer, it's about undocumented youth in general or our parents.

The "perfect DREAMer" image only privileges individuals who are positioned to make substantial contributions to U.S. society but leaves behind those who want to make contributions that society views as less notable. There is also no room for individuals to make mistakes or learn from poor choices. The "good moral character" clause is an immigration law requirement imposed on undocumented immigrants. The clause positions them in a precarious space, as they have to be always aware of their surroundings and contexts, in fear that they will be caught in the wrong place at the wrong time. Many of the individuals in this study have learned that activism is no longer about them or the DREAM Act; activism has become a much broader issue. Yahaira admits that at one point in her life, the focus of her activism was about the DREAM Act, but her experiences with nonprofit organizations and involvement with politics has shifted her consciousness, as she states,

I used to think, when I started advocating for the DREAM Act I was still in this very, very much pull yourself up by your bootstraps mentality. The DREAM Act is only going to help you get a pass to legalization. It isn't going to get your family out of poverty, it isn't going to stop brown people getting arrested, you know, it isn't going to stop other people getting detained, and it isn't going to stop domestic violence in our communities, or crime, or third grade reading levels for 16-year-olds. The DREAM Act doesn't fix any of that.

Yahaira's critical thinking has pushed immigration issues to intersect with other societal concerns. At some point, some of these students start to critique the legislation drafted to benefit undocumented students and move toward a heightened critical legal consciousness where they see themselves as revolutionaries, visionaries, humanitarians, and social justice educators beyond immigration and beyond helping only DREAMers. Jorge explains this most eloquently by stating,

I don't think I can only do immigration-related stuff because in order to solve it, you have to solve other issues, too. It's not a one-thing-only. So I also try to work with other organizations, trying to bring them to the same point that I'm trying to make to fight really for what's needed and tackle all the issues at once.

The criticalness comes along as students process their place within the movement and question the measures they must take in order to continue activist work. Not all students spoke of arriving at a juncture at which they begin to think critically about the injustices within the movement. Yahaira and Marco were two who spoke about their shifting perspectives. These critics come with introspection and critiques of themselves within the movement. The following section discusses Yahaira's experience with oppression within the movement and navigating self-care. It also discusses Marco's perspective about his activist work in relation to furthering the immigration agenda.

Critical Legal Consciousness

Yahaira is the most seasoned activist in this study; without question, her extensive time as an activist has resulted in personal growth. She made a reference articulating that the "movement" can be the love of your life, but it can also break your heart. She brought up an event that truly impacted her viewpoint about the movement:

I dealt with the, with patriarchy and I did bring it up. I brought it up and it was dismissed. I brought it up and I said, 'Look, this is not a boys' club.' … I was basically told, that's not true. And then later on I knew that they were meeting with a bunch of men about things that other people should've have been included, and the other people meaning women. Or, for example, talking about queerness and how queer issues needed to be included in the work that we were doing, and having a straight person tell me, well we can't do that because if we do that it's going to alienate the churches, particularly like the Catholic Dioceses. And me going, are you kidding me right now? Like, A, we've been organizing together; B, we keep talking about how we're not like these other organizations that throw people under the bus, and here we are throwing people under the bus. I'm here in the middle of the fucking night doing this work alongside you; it's not some random-ass person. And even if it was a random-ass person, just because you don't know them doesn't mean you get to throw them under the bus. And so like even confronting it and then having to have conversations to basically, where we had to make our case. Like having to make the case to make sure that the queer voice is included.

Yahaira's experience exemplifies the tension between differing ideologies and values within the undocumented student movement. These instances of oppression often result in the founding of new organizations, which can be more inclusive of other salient identities. Gender and sexual identities have been issues in social movements, and while dismantling power dynamics is one way to promote equity within social movements, women and queer individuals have to continue to voice their experiences of exclusion in order for change to occur. In recent years, women have been on the front lines of the undocumented youth movement. When the history of this particular social movement is written, one can only hope that by illuminating oppression among community organizing, we acknowledge the work that was accomplished by women and other marginalized identities. Unveiling these occurrences of exclusion within social movements also presents activists as imperfect human beings, disclosing how social movements and organizations are microcosms of the social inequities within U.S. society. It is through these imperfections that individuals begin to understand that it is necessary to work on equity within the movement with the same magnitude used to address human rights for immigrants.

Navigating Self-Care

The notion of self-care, while important to unpack, was not readily spoken about among the participants in this study. Yahaira advocates taking time to understand oneself as a social activist by questioning and analyzing oneself in relationship to the movement. She states,

I believe, if you don't take that time to analyze, and reevaluate, and see where you are, and who you are as opposed to when you started and where you want to go as a person. I think it's really easy to lose yourself and not know who you are. And I think that when you see that you're 27, and you're planning to live to be 100, which is totally my goal, and you plan to do revolutionary work for the rest of your life, you have to pace yourself. It isn't a sprint; it's a marathon. And if you go at it at a sprint, it's going to kill you, and it's going to make you extremely unhappy. And if I plan to be in this work for the rest of my life, then I have, it's a push and pull type thing, you know, it's an ebb and flow. Sometimes it's, go at it all force, and then sometimes it's retreat, enjoy the calm, let it be, reevaluate, reassess, and then pick up the work again in a different space, in a different way that continues to push you and help you grow as an individual.

This consciousness has prompted Yahaira to think longitudinally about her activist work and the importance of taking time for self in the process. She also mentions how imperative it is for social activists to listen to their bodies. She describes a critical point by stating,

Immigration is broader than yourself, you know? Like if you're an organizer, if you're a person that's in community and you're seeing all of the shit that people are dealing with every day, it becomes so much bigger than yourself, right? And we just get so caught up in that, in the love of community, and this love of making sure that our loved one is safe, and taken care of, and that they have this possibility to pursue things, and to be happy, and to be treated justly and fairly. And we take it upon ourselves to try to bring that about, I feel ... for me, I just got to a point of being tired. It's like being in tune to my body and how my body responds to things and situations. And then saying, I don't really like how this feels in my body, and I don't really want this to continue feeling this way in my body. So what am I going to do to make sure that I don't have these feelings anymore, like these physical feelings? And I just think culturally we've been taught to move away from that, from listening to our body.

Physical and emotional impacts related to the work of social activists ring true in this context but are perhaps not openly discussed among the undocumented activists. Yahaira highlights how one's body is used to heal others and that putting the needs of others first can have a biological effect on how one's body responds to witnessing trauma and injustices not only inside the community but also in detention centers.

Challenging Mainstream Politics

Another example of critical legal consciousness is shifting activist work to agitate current political and social systems by challenging the bureaucracy of politics and politicians. During our interview discussion, I inquired about a Facebook page administered by Marco called "Illegals for Romney." While it was intended to be humorous, he also discussed the importance of disrupting the common discourse that one political party would be more favorable to immigration issues than the other. He explains,

> I mean part of it was the absurdism and the comedy to it. Because I mean I think a lot of people did speak out about it, and I think we wanted to point toward why people, even so-called allies, are supportive of immigrants still thinking about it as a two-party system where one party is right, one party's not. Or why are people's mentalities wrapped around so much of who wins the next election when 1,200 people are being deported every day and funding for that machine doesn't seem to be stopping irrespective of who's in office, and might be worse under the Democratic administration. So we're trying to—I mean I think in a very creative, icky, and immature way kind of trying to point to that, and trying to say that a lot of the big money D.C. advocacy groups are funded by deep pockets of people within the Democratic Party that are interested in power and not necessarily foremost justice for the immigrant community. We should never lose sight of that because that makes our political analysis much more weak when we think that one party is any better because really we should be pushing both parties to be more humane and sensitive and not playing to Democrats. I mean I'm not saying no one really has the authority or the legitimacy to say that we'll deliver the Latino vote. But even if we could, we shouldn't say that because I think both parties should always be wanting to compromise with the needs of the immigrant community and not the other way around. So I think part of that was that critique …

Marco makes a tremendous point about how both political parties have positioned the issue of immigration to court the Latino vote, and both political parties are implicated in trying to use this issue to garner political power rather than acting to eliminate the inhumane injustices inflicted on the immigrant community. Under the Obama administration, more undocumented immigrants have been deported than under previous administrations, which has gotten President Obama dubbed "the Deporter-in-Chief," a testament that in the two-party system politics has prevailed over human will and the needs of people.

Reflection

Like the Chicana/o movement of the 1960s, the struggle for equity and justice for undocumented immigrants in the U.S. is complex. In many ways, the Chicana/o and the undocumented youth movements mirror one another: both struggled with collective and conflicting ideologies, which debunks one unifying voice or representation of the movement. The spirit of radical politics of the Chicana/o movement is illustrated in the strategic nature of infiltration of detention centers by undocumented youth. Parallels can also be made with exclusionary practices within both movements. Chicana feminism surged as a result of Chicana women reevaluating their own positions and beliefs, which were often incongruent with the Chicanos' dominant notions of gender roles (Garcia, 1989). Patriarchy, homophobia, and economic class are examples of three intersecting injustices that illuminate the tensions experienced within these two social movements. However, even though U.S.-born Latinas/os are also targets of anti-immigration policies, in most cases their legal status is a level of privilege and protection from deportation. Undocumented immigrant youth make democratic claims for equity and inclusion but operate as political subjects outside the system (Galindo, 2012).

The direct and indirect forms of civil disobedience can be found in both movements, yet the friction between both U.S.-born Latinas/os and undocumented immigrants perhaps stems from voice and representation. Historically, Mexican Americans have expressed their disdain for lenient immigration policies, claiming those policies may impede their own way of life but they developed strong solidarity connections through economic and ethnic commonalities (Gutiérrez, 1991). Recently, the matriarch of the Chicana/o movement, Dolores Huerta, expressed her support for President Obama's strategy to wait until after the 2014 mid-term elections for action on comprehensive immigration reform:

> 'We have to look at the big picture and don't get caught up in saying we want it now,' she said, referring to action on immigration. 'We've been waiting—we are a community that can wait. And we have to have faith in our president, because the Republicans have shown their hand. We know what they want to do.' (cited in Nevarez, 2014)

This statement is symbolic of the conflicting tactics used for social change that undermine the essence of the Chicana/o movement. Many of the students in this study have unveiled political allegiances that do not translate into political power or voice and have developed sophisticated means for agitating the system. It is often assumed that U.S.- born Latina/o politicians will stand in solidarity on immigration issues, which is far from the reality. It is most disheartening that a heroine like Dolores Huerta, one the most influential labor leaders in the U.S., who was at the forefront of civil unrest and understands issues of poverty and justice, uses her political capital to maintain the status quo. Cultivating a shared ideology to build cross-status coalitions is recommended in order to increase effectiveness (Enriquez, 2014). Conflict is inevitable in social movements; however, unpacking differing power levels and privileges among group members can strengthen the entirety of coalitions (Enriquez, 2014). It is equally imperative to question who has legitimacy to speak for or represent undocumented immigrants.

The individuals in this study came to be activists for different reasons and in a variety of ways. Some needed to find information about themselves and their experiences, some needed a community and support in order to heal from the stigma of their legal status, but most needed to act. For most of the participants, social activism is part of their personal mantra, individual philosophies, and lifestyle. They are perhaps different individuals because their social activism continues to be transformed by other individuals, social contexts, and actions. These actions are diverse and fluid. From community educators to detention center infiltrators, each action that agitates the system represents that a layer of fear has been stripped away, that empowered knowledge has been harnessed, and that the fragments of dignity have been pieced together. These visionaries, humanitarians, and revolutionaries envision a world in which justice for undocumented immigrants would translate into equity for all marginalized individuals.

I continue to ponder the notion of social activist self-care. This issue is particularly interesting to me because it was rarely discussed as habitual practice. I also wonder whether the concept of self-care for undocumented individuals is privilege-laden. I am reminded of Marco's words about the luxury of being able to make meaning of being undocumented and unafraid. It is easy for individuals to think about the importance of self-care if they are operating under the notion that self-care is accessible and affordable. Outside the realm of the collegiate context, many do not have access to health care or mental health resources. So, if activists intuitively sense something is wrong with their body, where do they seek assistance? After activists have spent weeks in a detention holding center, how do they heal from this trauma? These basic rights are human rights. What every American citizen must also understand is that under our current system, under our inhumane practices, and our lack of leadership to address this issue in a human and just way, America continues to hurt these individuals. American practices and polices are implicated. In many ways, these activists, much like their Chicana/o counterparts, are trying to find a way to live in a society that has created every conceivable barrier. I can only imagine how differently the educational pathways for Chicanas/os would be constructed if Sal Castro, Paula Crisostomo, Moctesuma Esparza, the United Mexican American Students (UMAS), and the Brown Berets were advised to "wait and be patient."

Chapter Six

Cultivating Undocumented and Unafraid as a Form of Resistance to Legal Violence ... *"We fight, sometimes, for single issues, but as human beings we aren't single issues"*

During my freshman year of college, I remember stepping on to the neatly manicured lawns of my predominately white college campus, with the usual measures of hopes, anxiety, and fears. As I interacted with my fellow college mates, I felt the sidelong glances at my appearance, as if I was being studied. I was caught off guard when I was first asked, "What are you?" I felt inadequate because I had rarely thought about that question. When I answered, "I'm Mexican," my response was met with another face of confusion. My white skin and light eyes did not neatly fit the normative assumptions behind what was considered "Mexican," which angered me and prompted me to journey on my own meaning-making process of my ethnicity. Who am I?

Attempting to find an identity development model that speaks to the experiences of individuals without legal status is like to trying to fit a square peg into a round hole. While I discuss different foundational identity models in this chapter, none gives credence to the political and contextual nuances that come with identifying as "undocumented and unafraid" under the auspices of social and political contexts. This chapter examines foundational student identity theories and their shortcomings with regard to their applicability to undocumented individuals. I introduce how the notion of legal violence applies to identity development. I also discuss how the notion of undocumented and un-afraid is complex by unmasking the fluidity of its meaning.

Foundational Identity Formation Models

Student identity development has posited college as the ideal space for students to grapple with and make sense of their identity. Foundational identity scholars (Chickering & Reisser, 1993; Erikson, 1968; Josselson, 1987; Marcia, 1966) depicted developmental phases, stages, and pro-cesses in which students take into account their identities and how they interact within the context of society and their social positions. Erick-son (1968) in particular contends that changes in identity are an out-come produced by the ways in which students negotiate inner conflicts about their identities within a context that offers a supportive environ-ment. Marcia (1966) and Josselson (1987) both note the importance of exploration of identity as a way to move beyond identities that have been assumed before students arrive at college. Both of these models argue that students cannot commit to an identity without meaningful exploration. While "conflict" and "crisis" are words that describe the event in which students grapple with their inner selves, the authors fail to explain how the commitment occurs, how environmental con-texts factor into this decision, and what particular action or behaviors are exhibited after commitment is made to a particular identity. One known limitation of foundational theories is that many are grounded in the experiences of white men and women and race or racism is often not interrogated in the identity development process (Jones & Abes, 2013; Patton, McEwen, Rendón, & Howard Hamilton, 2007). Two iden-tity theories serve as useful tools when examining the experiences of undocumented immigrants: social identity and the reconceptualized model of multiple dimensions of identity.

Social Identity

Children may feel positive or indifferent about themselves depending on their environment and family upbringing. This notion coincides with current immigration research (Portes & Rambaut, 2006). The focus of social identity (Deaux, 1993; Hardiman & Jackson, 1997) is on how group membership shapes and impacts one's self-perception. The social identity model posits five different stages of social identity development: (1) naïve or no social consciousness, in which children are born as empty vessels and without knowledge of their identity until they begin to gain information from social institutions such as family, school, and religion; (2) acceptance, in which individuals actively or passively adopt these messages about their identity; (3) resistance, in which negotiation occurs and individuals receive new knowledge and reexamine their roles and beliefs that may collude with old values and information; (4) redefinition, in which they make sense of their own identity by surrounding themselves with members of the same social group; and (5) internalization, in which they incorporate their social identity into everyday life. The social identity model is helpful in interrogating the experiences of undocumented immigrants. While linear in nature, this model is helpful for understanding the process by which one is shaped and impacted by new information. The reconceptualized model of multiple dimensions of identity sheds light on the interaction between context and identity.

Reconceptualized Model of Multiple Dimensions of Identity (RMMDI)

Susan Jones and Elisa Abes' research on multiple dimensions of identity speaks to interactions between core self (personal identities) along with social identities (race, class, gender, sexual orientation) within a lived context (sociocultural conditions, family background, and life experiences). Their research took into account the foundational theories of student development, research on underrepresented groups, and the distinctions between personal and social identities. While citing limitations of a small sample size, capturing the graphic representation of fluidity with the model, and a lack of nuance to identity saliency beyond social identities, Susan Jones and Elisa Abes worked with Marylu McEwen to reconceptualize MMDI. Named reconceptualized model of multiple dimensions (RMMDI), these scholars added focus to the meaning making process of identity development by incorporating Kegan's self evolutionary theory and Baxter Magolda's self authorship as way to decipher meaning (Abes, Jones, & McEwen, 2007; Jones & Abes, 2013). Other forms of the MMDI and RMMDI frameworks include the use of intersectional model of multiple dimensions of identity to examine the interlocking and intersecting systems of power and oppressions. Critical race theory and queer theory can also be applied to this framework to situate saliency of identity and the filtering of contextual influences. To date, none of the foundational and contemporary models of student development theory has been used to examine the experiences of undocumented immigrants. I intentionally incorporate how social and political contexts impact how undocumented individuals incorporate knowledge that informs their legal consciousness; particularly how one makes meaning of their identities under the curtain of legal violence.

Legal Violence

Cecilia Menjívar and Leisy Abrego (2012) articulate how legal violence impacts the everyday lives of immigrants living in U.S. society. This concept refers to the "harmful effects of the law that can obstruct and derail immigrants' paths" (p. 1383). Two other types of violence inform these authors' discussion: structural and symbolic violence. Structural violence emphasizes how the overall system perpetuates systemic inequities through implicit or explicit exploitation of immigrants in the labor force, in the educational system, and even by barring them from resources that would assist in upward mobility or incorporation into U.S. mainstream society. Symbolic violence refers to the normalization of inequities and how those who are targets of these violent occurrences begin to accept their position in the social order. Those who inflict violence also find normalcy in perpetuating these inequities. In other words, when you pass dehumanizing laws and policies against undocumented immigrants, or bar them from accessing higher education, it further justifies treating immigrants inhumanly. Jessica, from Arizona, illustrates this context as she describes how she navigates her legal status after the passage of Senate Bill 1070:

> It was basically targeting people of color. And it was a little bit difficult because you couldn't come out as you wanted. Before, I was saying, 'I don't have papers, and I was born in Mexico,' but now I have to second-guess myself because you don't know how much power the other person who could just call the police and pull you into the process for deportation because of this law.

Legal violence aims at specific laws and policies that prohibit immigrants from economic and social mobility while also impeding psychological wellness. I argue that participants who self-identify as undocumented and unafraid are resisting legal violence. However, I also argue that some legal violence is somewhat internalized among the participants in this study. The next section highlights what it means to be undocumented and unafraid.

Social Construction and Context of Legal Consciousness

How participants in this study constructed themselves and their legal status varied by prior experiences with their legal status during their formative years, the context of other salient identities, and how legality and legal consciousness are self-constructed behind the curtain of legal violence. For the purposes of this study, legal consciousness is defined as the process in which an individual's lived experiences and self are constructed, shaped, and influenced by the law or legal norms (Silbey, 2005). Abrego (2011) discusses two strands within legal consciousness: "with the law" and "against the law" (p. 341). Undocumented immigrants fall into the "against the law" category. They actively try to understand and navigate their place in society while simultaneously silencing, masking, and negotiating who they are in order to fit in "with the law." In my attempt to expand the notion of legal consciousness, I make a parallel with mestiza consciousness to demonstrate its fluidity and how a heightened legal consciousness is formed to critique and resist legal violence through social activism.

During our conversation, Marco presented three different levels of making meaning regarding undocumented and unafraid, public disclosure, political action, and philosophical meanings. He explains public disclosure as "being honest enough with myself and trusting the relationships that I had built that I could be publicly undocumented with my status and say that to my closest friends and support networks." At the public disclosure level, dropping the fear of deportation is also evident. Yovany explains, "It's being [able] to say, 'I'm not afraid to tell America what I am and hope America will come to understand my position.'" It also means not having to live in the shadows and being unafraid of the responses from those holding opposing opinions. The next level involves the participants' using personal narratives as educational and political tools to encourage others.

The political action presents undocumented and unafraid as a political tool coinciding with the action and intentionality behind community organizing and public disclosure. Marco states,

> I think I've learned this from just working on deportation cases, that being publicly undocumented, and trusting your relationship, and building up your social networks, by telling people this very, very deep truth about you, it's like the most proactive step that one can take to stop the deportation before even being in proceedings. So building up all of those reservoirs of social networks.

The social networks that are constructed from connecting with other undocumented individuals is one way in which these individuals are able to mobilize and understand themselves more deeply not only through the networks of individuals but also about the process and system, and how to re-shift their consciousness. It is during this process of action that undocumented community activists become the holders of knowledge and become able to transform their own communities. Sarai describes this phenomenon:

> Other community members are looking for those resources, they're just hungry for knowledge and when we offer services, they're the ones that are coming toward us, we're not trying to find them in the shadows, they're coming out of the shadows and they're coming to these organizations and we're trying to plug them in, into the world of community organizing.

Community empowerment is central to shaping legal consciousness. Jessica participates in ScholarshipsA-Z, an immigration advocacy organization in Tucson, Arizona, which connects undocumented students to resources for college. She discusses how she teaches and supports aspiring college students to research information and resources "so they can learn from the process and teach it to someone else." The actions taken by these participants have helped to liberate others from their own fears, develop confidence, and bring potential opportunity and hope to their communities. With this said, context must be interrogated when examining its impacts on legal consciousness. The context of Arizona posed many challenges for Jessica. The onset of SB 1070 brought a wealth of educational opportunities in the form of workshops and other resources to help in the drive to understand the impact of this law in the context of one's legal rights. Undocumented students also became more vocal and started to disclose their legal status, which increased anti-immigrant sentiments in her community. She recalls, "More people started to come out and they [anti-immigration people] started to see that we were not the same color as them and that we were coming into power." She ends by stating, "It's based on the white supremacy that has always existed." Even as Jessica has increased her own legal consciousness and uses her activism to resist white supremacy, she does so in a state ideology that blatantly reproduces white supremacy through its anti-immigration laws.

Marco invokes a philosophical stance, which requires introspection and depth into critiquing and resisting legal violence. He states,

> For me it's really saying that an undocumented immigrant is very much a threat to the current institutions and underlying powers that exist because people prove that this country isn't a democracy and proved that capitalism has these evil ramifications. I think the reason why so many people when they first hear our stories feel sorry or bad, because they themselves feel irreconcilable with the curriculum within the system, because we are all at some level implicated by it. And so in our own complacency we have upheld the current system that terrorizes undocumented immigrants and therefore the listener can no longer avoid that reality. So by saying you're undocumented and unafraid you're very much assaulting the whole system of reality that has threatened your family for such a long time.

This example of heightened legal consciousness manifests in how Marco has made meaning of his legal status behind the curtain of legal violence, which has formulated his personal philosophy about his own self-perception. This critique and active resistance form perhaps one definition of undocumented and unafraid, but even more it differentiates the deeper, nuanced thinking about the lived experience of undocumented immigrants in U.S. society. With that said, it is important to highlight that not all participants regarded their status at this heightened level; thus, one is able to exist and fluctuate along the undocumented and unafraid consciousness spectrum.

While Marco and a few other participants had established solid foundational philosophies behind their legal status and activism work, I assumed that everyone in this study would embrace undocumented and unafraid as a social identity and political statement. Interestingly, some students did not want to be defined by their legal status. For instance, David had a different perspective about his legal status as a social identity. He posits,

> So for me it's kind of just been more of kind of stepping in and out of those circles, if you will. Because I definitely don't want to see myself as kind of perpetrating my own status, like constantly calling myself undocumented and I think it creates a psychological handicap. I think it would damage me psychologically in the long term and it would kind of make me feel resentful for my parents' actions, for them being in the situation. So I'd rather just focus on the progress that can be made and the progress that has been made, right, at the state level, the federal level, but also locally. So I'd rather just focus on who I am as a person, as a whole.

Perhaps this compartmentalization of his legal status is one survival strategy for dealing with the psychological impacts of legal violence. Not embracing one's legal status does equate to lack of pride and commitment to the immigrant youth movement. Legal status may not be as salient as other identities, but not anchoring one's identity to one's legal status can be a coping mechanism, a way to protect against pain. Others students expressed, "I am more than my status" or "I want to be seen as a human being," statements that perhaps are commentaries about the larger system and the psychological harm that comes from living in the shadows. This is not to assume that these students do not have self-agency, but rather are operating under a system that has attacked their existence.

It is imperative to delineate a distinction between heightened legal consciousness and understanding legal status as an identifier. Juan provides a wonderful analogy when discussing how he views his status:

> I think it's [legal status] more of like an umbrella because it's over me but I can't ignore it and I need it because it's made me who I am, it's taught me so much but I don't embrace it so much ... like it's a status. And it could change tomorrow.

While legal status has shaped the identity of these individuals, embracing their legal status would communicate affirmation of its place in U.S. society. To have a heightened legal consciousness does not equate to embracing one's legal status, but rather interrogating the systems that perpetuate legal violence in immigrant communities, and working toward healing and resolving inequities within the immigration system. A heightened legal consciousness is also the act of questioning the root cause of why legal violence continues to thrive, prompting one to create transformational change individually and within communities.

There are many layers to identifying as undocumented and unafraid. At the heart of this identity process is the acknowledgment, disclosure of legal status, and use of narratives as a means to push back on a system that has inflicted pain and shame on the undocumented community. The participants in this study do not like their legal status, they do not embrace being unable to live fully in U.S. society, but they appreciate and acknowledge that their legal status has provided them with social and cultural capital. This currency has given these participants agency to act, to use their voices, and to challenge the system. However, how legal status shapes one's identity is also influenced by context and other multiple identities.

Intersectionality with a *Trenza* Twist

Intersectionality is the axis in which multiple social identities meld together to form a new identity that can be both privileged and oppressed. Kimberle Crenshaw (1991) posits that inspecting multiple forms of subordination allows for deeper analysis of how structural systems of oppression are reproduced within the social world in order to displace, disempower, and disenfranchise people. Francisca González (1998) coined the term *trenzas de identidades múltiples* to depict the fluidity with which identity and cultural knowledge can be interwoven with "cultural morality, life energy, transformation of vitality and desire, spirituality, and personal and societal relational behaviors" (p. 89). To theorize legality, I use *trenzas de identidades múltiples* to present how participants in this study define their multiple identities along with their legal status to create their own undocumented and unafraid epistemologies and cultural intuition. These identities are informed by systems of oppression and societal contexts. The following are excerpts from participants who articulate how their identities are juxtaposed with their legal status.

Embracing Undocuqueerness

Yahaira identified as fem queer. Her journey to unraveling and making sense of her gender and sexual identity, alongside her activism work within the undocumented immigrant movement, was a lengthy and difficult process. She describes the way she appears physically as normative, putting her in both a privileged and challenging position. People often presume that because she identifies as fem queer, navigating societal spaces is an easier process; however, "passing" often makes her invisible within queer spaces. At times, she has to justify her queerness—another layer she must navigate in addition to her legal status. She details,

> Yeah, and then it goes without saying, being, living at an intersection of two identities, it's the same thing, it's like, the DREAM Act is going to legalize my status, but is it going to let me marry my partner? Is it going to let me have

a family? Is it going to let me adopt when I want to adopt when I'm older? Just like personally. And see that we fight, sometimes, for single issues, but as human beings we aren't single issues. Like there isn't just one thing that affects us, and if we fix that thing we're automatically better. But the thing is, like I said, you only come, I only came to those conclusions by really being introspective in thinking. But when you're working yourself to the bone you sometimes don't have time to think about those things.

This statement braids together her sexual identity, social class, and gender along with her legal status to demonstrate that her lived realities are interconnected to the broader context of social equity. She points out how problematizing only her legal status does not absolve all the equity woes in the immigrant world.

During our conversation, unpacking the notion of "undocuqueer" was equally important to the discussion of identity. While Yahaira felt that "undocuqueer" was a political term, it was also a lived experience and made reference to how undocuqueer spaces were created within the context of the undocumented youth movement. She recalls,

So undocuqueer wasn't there, you know, and we created that space, and now that space is there. So things were playing at the same time, the patriarchy and the queer issues. Seems like one of those was fully embraced and addressed and space was made so that that identity could be acknowledged and respected and embraced. And that was successful, it's been very successful. How willing people are to call out the patriarchy in the movement, I would say it's much less. We've definitely not moved the needle on that front I don't feel. I would say that it has moved in the sense that visually, if you look at who the people in the lead positions are, you see a lot more females. And so movement-wise you see them. But there is no discussion about patriarchy as an issue within the movement. Compared to queerness and how it's talked about ... I think, for example, when people talk about including undocuqueer women into spaces and it's all undocuqueer men that are figuring out how to include undocuqueer women into spaces.

The creation of inclusive spaces is derived from challenging dominant notions of gender and sexual identities. However, evident in Yahaira's statement, even within these inclusive spaces, issues of patriarchy or other inequities are unaddressed. While seemingly the increase among women in leadership positions may perhaps be viewed as a remedy to patriarchy, it halts tackling other issues of inequalities, which often permeate within organizational culture.

Working Class and Legal Status

Angelica attends graduate school at an elite private college in an urban setting and her social work courses allow her to delve into her own social identities. In one of her graduate courses she was asked to reflect on a couple of her identities: one that was privileged and another that was not. She reflected on the fact that she was at an elite school, and how to some, her access to college offered her some privilege. She also identified most with her experiences as an undocumented immigrant, but just recently unpacked her social class as a salient identifier through her contact with an artist she recently met who positioned his working-class background as an asset. This critical event led her to think more deeply about her own working-class background. She recalls,

I'm becoming more cognizant of, that I don't embrace other identities like my social class. I don't talk very much about it. But I am very much aware of it. And so I think by listening to that artist it was an opportunity to reflect on it and I guess it's something that I accept, I don't think of with pride, or I don't think of with shame, but I just, I see it a little bit—I'm sort of distant from it. But I have been aware that, I mean I attended one of the worst schools in New York City and, and I think it still seems somewhat surreal that, I don't know from just my background, and the type of education that I had, especially primary education, which was not the best, and being here I, I wonder if I'm at the right place. Or I just wonder how it happened because it seems so strange that I'm not the typical student who should be, or who normally attends the [elite private college], but someone of just a very humble background ... I think what I've realized is that I, that I want to be able to embrace it and talk about it, and admit, yes, that I grew up in a poor neighborhood, I mean I think it would be hard for me to say that I'm poor, because both my parents are, thankfully, are both working, and they're helping me. But I mean we're not privileged, we're not wealthy. My parents have worked extremely hard. But, because of their work, because of their sacrifice, we do live in a neighborhood that's secure. We don't have to worry about that. They've been able to help me as much as they can be able to go to school. And so I think I'm still somewhat reconciling my, my background with the achievements, both of my family and their sacrifices, and my achievements and, and seeing that it's a process that's even developing now. I don't know if I've really come to a conclusion or that I've reconciled, but it's something that's ongoing, at least for now.

Much of Angelica's consciousness of her social class is perhaps heightened by her new context at a private elite college. The noticeable social class disparities have caused her to interrogate her own educational journey and how perhaps lack of legal status has contributed to her access to low-resourced educational pathways. In many ways, Angelica also complicates her own academic accolades by questioning, "I'm not suppose to be here" or "Students like me don't normally access private elite schools," which is a common tendency for many first-generation and low-income students. Because this subpopulation of college students is not readily represented or visible within the fabric of higher education, they consider themselves the exception rather than the "rule" or the norm. Angelica demonstrates this statement by expressing,

> I mean I'm certainly aware of being at [elite private college] that most of the students there are white, are middle class or upper middle class. And so I think at times I definitely feel very lonely, being Latina, being undocumented, and coming from a working class [background].

Spiritual Foundations and Legal Status

Spiritual epistemology is used to "understand spirituality as that essence that moves us, that makes us whole, that gives us strength, then essentially, spirituality gives us hope" (Galván, 2006, p. 173). Spirituality can be used as a source of strength to endure the everyday lived experiences of undocumented immigrants. By tapping into ancestral and spiritual teaching and learning, individuals are able to make meaning of their life's purpose, gain strength to hurdle challenges, and develop strong community connections and support (Galván, 2006). It is through this process that individuals become empowered and resilient (Galván, 2006; Villenas, 2005). Religiosity was a common thread among the majority of the participants who used their spiritual epistemologies in different ways. Jaen, from New Mexico, discussed extensively how his spirituality ties into his activist work and how he navigates his legal status. During our discussions, Jaen attributed his success and his acquired blessing to his faith. His ability to put faith above his legal status has given him a greater purpose in life.

> I think that one of the reasons why I identify myself as a Christian is because I, because I grew up in a Christian home. And also, I had a strong belief in God even before I knew that I was undocumented. So, and, because when I found out that I was undocumented was when I tried to apply for college, the community college. And it's a funny story because I went back to my mom and I told her, 'Mom, what am I going to do, what am I going to provide? They're asking me for a Social Security number in order to take classes.' And she said, 'You know what, God will provide. God will facilitate the means for you to go to school.' And so I was on the, that God moves in different ways in our lives. And in my vocation, in my experience, all I had to do was trust in Him. I really didn't worry before, after knowing that I wasn't going to be able to go to school. I didn't really worry about it because I knew that something better was there for me. And so, really thinking about how God will never leave you alone, will never leave you or forsake you, or something that it was, that was really, that's really, that I have in my head all the time. And so two weeks later I received a letter through the mail saying that I was accepted into the [name of college]. So I thought, God is awesome [laughter]. And I've always, throughout my college career I've always thought that it is God the one that gives me all the opportunities that I have now. And it's not through my works that I'm able to accomplish all this stuff, but God who is with me. And so that's how I was able to develop an identity as a son of God, and also knowing that my immigration status, that's something that I can't do anything about.

In this case, Jaen's mother passed on her spiritual epistemologies in teaching him to lean on his faith for strength and empowerment. Most interesting was that Jaen's faith helped him cope with his legal status. Unlike some of his counterparts in this study, he was less stressed because he placed his faith in something much greater than his legal status. Prior research (Pérez - Huber, 2010) positioned spirituality as cultural wealth for undocumented students and viewed it as an additional asset-based navigational tool. It is equally important to note that Jaen viewed his Christian faith as a point of privilege and rarely spoke of his spiritual identity within his undocumented activism space because he feared being viewed as imposing his personal beliefs on others. While Jaen's legal status was validated within the undocumented activist movement, he chose to keep his faith hidden within this context. He would rather demonstrate his faith though his actions instead of his words. This interaction between his faith identity and legal status is most prevalent in his activist work. He contends,

> What I learned about myself would be to not depend on only my strengths but also acknowledge that without the people who are being helped or who are being served, we can't really do anything. So that's something that I have learned that is to not think that I'm the only one or that I, that I'm independent but also taking into consideration that I'm here to serve, to serve the other people, to serve my community, and to serve other students.

Jaen connects his life's purpose, his faith in a higher power, and how he executes and works with helping others. In retrospect, his faith served as an important coping tool not only to survive but also to overcome many challenges and hardships his legal status produced. His faith has provided a way of living and resisting, rather than merely surviving.

Reading Race and Legal Status

Identities such as national origin, language, citizenship, and legal status are some important distinctions that negate homogeneity among Latinas/os. These cultural elements are also racial markers that position Latinas/os as a racialized ethnicity. (Alcoff, 2006; Aranda & Rebollo-Gil, 2004; De Genova & Ramos-Zayas, 2003; Grosfoguel, 2004; Maldonado & Licona, 2007; Muñoz & Maldonado, 2011; Oboler, 1995). In an earlier co-authored article on the experiences of undocumented Mexican women (Muñoz & Maldonado, 2011), we found that examples of minimization of race challenge the homogeneity of Latinas/os and how students read race within their contextualized surroundings and experiences. This section adds to the notion of reading race within social contexts and life experiences. Most of the students become race conscious when they start to examine their schooling experiences. Jorge, a student in engineering, states,

Well, definitely I'm a more conscious student and I tend to critique the system a lot. When you're inside in the classroom, you notice demographics in one particular major. I'm an engineering student, so the great majority are white males, and then you look at your own high school and see most of your peers—the ones who made it—are in technical colleges. But most of my peers went into the workforce. I mean, they don't really stand a chance competing with these college kids from really good schools.

As indicative of the low numerical representation of Latinos in Jorge's engineering courses, he later theorizes that beyond status, Latinos are not encouraged to pursue higher education. Ariel had similar experiences in his prior schooling and concluded, "I think this has do to more with race than status."

Most of the participants discussed how their social context played a role in how they made meaning of their race and legal status. Alex describes his upbringing in the Coachella Valley as "a bubble in the desert." He explains,

It's half of the people are just white and then in some parts it's Latino and you can tell in geographies and also demographics, you know how that entails and how hard the roles, socioeconomically speaking, you have the rich people on one side and you have the poorest people on the other side. So going to school in the middle of the bubble, it was just interactional, how do I deal with white people, how do I deal with queer people that don't understand immigration.

His axis points of intersectionality are crisscrossed by race, class, legal status, and sexual orientation. In a broader sense, this testament also speaks to the intersectionality of immigration. Immigration is a poverty, race, feminist, and queer issue.

Each individual in this study has taken a journey that vastly differs from that of the others; therefore, there is no one definition of undocumented and unafraid. While I have attempted to articulate the essence of these experiences and the self-perceptions of these community activists, how each person has been socialized highlights the beauty, messiness, complexity, and the fluidity of multiple identities. Perhaps the participants in this study will regard what they read in this book as obsolete, as each will continue to be changed and transformed with each new experience, new people, and new context. Yahaira states,

> In getting to this point that I'm at now in how I identify, in how I view the world, in how I analyze it, in the kind of relationships that I build, like I don't think any of that would be possible if I hadn't gone through this journey, if I hadn't, if I hadn't gotten involved and done that kind of work where your heart aches, and your heart breaks and you have people question your motives. And when you're in a place where you're being questioned all the time, where your motives are being questioned, like you have to know what the hell you're doing, why you're doing it.

This keen advice illuminates the importance of introspection and the significance of pausing, thinking, and questioning. Who am I?

Reflections

Identity development for undocumented students is a complex process. The factor most salient to making meaning of their legal status was access to social networks, which heightened their legal consciousness. The knowledge gained about their legal consciousness was not only used to resist legal violence but also used to empower their communities. It is important to note that the levels of legal violence and access to social networks are contextualized according to state ideologies. Context plays an important role when interrogating the ways in which participants make meaning of their legal status. For instance, identifying as undocumented and unafraid in Arizona poses different challenges than it does for those who live in other states. This is not an attempt to position states as less or more favoring of undocumented immigrants. The navigational strategies of disclosure perhaps differ in accordance to context, which may shape their identities. For some, their legal status was a point of contention; while it served as a source of strength, some were actively trying to alter their legal status through their social activism. This tension may create a lack of allegiance to their legal status, unlike other salient identities. However, it is undeniable that their legal status has shaped their life experiences and juxtaposed it with their other identities.

Making meaning of their legal status also requires individuals to examine intersectionality with other identities such as race, spirituality, gender, sexual orientation, and social class. For the participants in this study, living without legal status not only allowed them to filter other identities through their legal status, but also allowed them to process how their legal status intersects with perhaps privileged identities. Alex's words—"how do I deal with white people and how do I make queer people understand immigration"—exemplify the struggle that undocumented individuals experience as both insider and outsider in a community. Most participants felt both a sense of membership and subordination within a social context, in part due to their legal status but more so because of the inequities across multiple identities. Evident in this study, other salient identities such as spirituality, sexual orientation, race, or class were also sources of strength and pride.

When reflecting on my own understanding of my ethnic identity, my own process was filled with liberation and heartbreak. Surrounded by walls of corn in rural Iowa, among the sea of Caucasian college students, my context provided a rude awakening to notions of inequities and racism. Yet, this context provided me tools to use to critically navigate my surroundings. While my ethnicity was often incongruent with the institutional culture of my university, I found niches and spaces where I found validation. In retrospect, as a Chicana professor who teaches student development theory, I have learned that there are few identity development models that truly speak to the college experiences of Latina/o students, and none addresses how legal status and critical legal consciousness shape identity development. How students make meaning of their salient identities is operationalized behind the curtain of their legal status and legal violence. By factoring their migration experiences, their local context, coming out as undocumented, along with their social networks and family/peer relationships, identity models for undocumented and unafraid activists can be constructed.

Finally, while not apparent in this chapter, the notion of identity privilege was mentioned as an important point. All participants in this study mentioned how some of their salient identities position them in spaces of privilege; it is also these acknowledgements and acts that add to a heightened critical legal consciousness.

Chapter Seven

From Undocumented to Becoming DACAmented ... *"I licked my card and it tastes like plastic, it doesn't taste like freedom"*

DACA Clinic Reflection: With a cup of hot coffee in hand, I arrive promptly at 8 a.m. at the middle school to set up for the DACA clinic, only to find 10 families awaiting our arrival at the front door. I quicken my pace to meet the rest of the volunteers inside the school while making eye contact with the little children, flashing them an excited smile. Inside the old cafeteria I find my DACA clinic teammates consisting of law school students, lawyers, Latino student organization members, and university and community members.

Once the tables, paperwork, and organizers are ready, the cafeteria quickly fills and is buzzing with voices. My first applicant, accompanied by his mother, sits down and sets an overflowing folder in the middle of our table. The mother looks unfazed by this process but the young man seems excited. During the inquiry process I hear a few particular questions ("How did you get here? Where was the point of entry?") that bring back a flood of memories for the mother. A bit sad and in pain, she tells me her story, which answers the majority of questions I was going to ask. The young man opens the brown folder and presents his birth certificate from Guanajuato and a laundry list of all his academic accolades, school activities, and community service recognition. He has no criminal record, wants to attend college, and "do something" with biology. I send him along to the exit table and know that his case should pass through. The day continues with many variations involving many kinds of documents, degrees of emotion, and complexities. I watch as many applicants exit the building excited, giddy, and eager to start a new phase of their lives. I watch, hopeful, and wishing they could have so much more.

The summer of 2012 was ripe for acts of civil disobedience. Recovering from the failure to pass the DREAM Act two years earlier, the upcoming presidential elections loomed. The promise of passing a comprehensive immigration reform bill during President Obama's first term was a political tactic used to sway the Latina/o votes toward the Democratic Party. Student and community activists began to occupy and demonstrate inside various Obama campaign headquarters in order not only to communicate their disapproval of the lack of action, but also to remind voters that immigration as a platform issue had not been resolved within Congress. It came as no surprise that on June 15, 2012, President Obama initiated Deferred Action for Childhood Arrivals (DACA). DACA is a temporary relief. It provides eligible undocumented immigrants the opportunity to obtain a two-year work permit without a pathway to legalization. This chapter provides a brief overview of the key findings from the National UnDACAmented Research Project and how these participants in this study make meaning of this new policy.

Assessment of DACA: The Two-Year Report

Professor Roberto Gonzales has been the leading expert in coordinating and researching the beneficiaries of DACA in order to understand and pinpoint not only the benefits of this policy but also its shortcomings. In a recent report (Gonzales & Bautista Chavez, 2014), a national survey collected by the National UnDACAmented Research Project retrieved responses from 2,684 DACA-eligible young adults, the largest data sample of this particular population. The key findings indicate that DACA recipients found opportunities through new employment, internships, and the ability to obtain driver's licenses, open bank accounts, and secure credit cards and health care. While the majority of the public takes these amenities for granted, DACAmented individuals are enjoying these opportunities and basic rights at a relatively older age compared with most individuals residing in the U.S. The greatest benefactors of DACA are undocumented individuals who have already obtained a bachelor's degree. DACA applicants were 1.5 times more likely to increase their earning capacity, using their college degree as an additional credential, than DACA applicants without a college degree.

The report also highlights various reasons DACA-eligible individuals are not applying for the program. The subsample of 244 respondents cite the $465 application fee, lack of knowledge about community resources, missing paperwork, or other legal factors as reasons for not applying for DACA. The respondents also mentioned the lack of trust in the federal government concerning the confidentiality of their personal information and awaiting better options for themselves as additional reasons.

The following are recommendations from this report with regard to how to support undocumented students through DACA: (1) Include expanding resources to serve the needs of DACA-eligible applicants who have not applied to the program because they may not have access to community resources or are unable to pay the application fee. (2) Make access to post-secondary education more seamless and obtainable by charging in-state tuition while opening federal and state financial aid to DACA recipients. (3) Create an intentional partnership with the existing workforce in order to provide job training, skills enhancement, and internship opportunities for community college–level DACA recipients, or those who have yet to access post-secondary education. (4) This recommendation aligns with many of my conversations with study participants: DACA should be viewed as a temporary solution to the greater issue, the legalization of 12 million undocumented individuals and relief for their family members.

During these interviews, DACA was a contentious topic in the media. I was curious to see how my study participants viewed this national policy and its potential impacts on their livelihoods. While the topic of DACA was not central to the study, it became an important topic of discussion as we conversed about how undocumented community activists made meaning of their newfound status. The following are excerpts about the application process, the meaning behind being DACAmented, and the rationale used for not applying for DACA.

The DACA Application Process

The application process for DACA is not only a monetary burden; it also takes an immense amount of time to gather the various documents required. This parallels Aurora Chang's (2011) notion of being "hyper-documented," a critique of the various ways in which accolades and college degrees legitimatize presence in the U.S. The DACA application is a form of hyperdocumentation in which applicants have to provide documentation of their continuing presence in the U.S. Some study participants mentioned that this was the most daunting part of the application process. Sarai received training in how to help others fill out their DACA applications. When it came time to apply for her own, she stated,

> I finally got to my application, and I asked my mom, she's like, you know, you're helping everyone else out, you should start on your application. It was like a little overwhelming. And it's actually a pretty long process of getting all the paperwork, finding everything. My application was relatively simple because I graduated and then I went to college right away, so I had a lot of documentation, but even then it's a lot of, a lot of paperwork to get through, and signed and copies [made]. Yeah, it's a little time consuming. But it's all worth it.

The application process differed for those who resided in the same area for years compared with those who moved various times throughout their upbringing. There was also a difference for those fortunate enough to access community entities that assisted in the process of filling out the application and resolving the fee. Jaen, in the process of applying for DACA, touches on this issue:

> You know, I'm in the process of applying for Deferred Action now. But I haven't applied. I haven't been able to apply. Thankfully some of the people at church were able to get a hold of a really great resource of an organization called New Mexico Law Access Center and they're going to be providing scholarships for two members of the church, or three members of the church, so they can apply for Deferred Action. That and also just, I guess taking my time to get all the information. I have to go to California to pick up some of

the stuff that I needed. And also some medical records that I needed from California.

While Jaen lived in only two states, many immigrants in the U.S. are transient. Making many moves within the U.S. may pose difficulties for some DACA-eligible individuals when trying to locate past documents such as school and medical records, costing time and additional money. For others, like Antonio, it was an easy application process:

> I mean if you have everything, all the documents that they require, you know, and you make it official, then it's, it's faster. But if you, if you find it hard for you to find like specific documents and you have a harder time to send it. But I sent mine right away and I did it online too, like, just uploaded the application and sent them to them. First, first how it works is, you'll send your application, they'll send you a letter and that letter has your code number, and then you have to submit that code when you go to your biometrics. And then, if you get approved, you'll wait for a couple months and then they'll send the documents.

For some of the participants in this study, waiting for DACA approval was a nerve-wracking process. Individuals place a great deal of trust in the U.S. government as they expose themselves to the very entity that continues to terrorize immigrants and separate families. Juan, from Florida, explains how social media have been powerful tools during the DACA application process and disclosed a Facebook page solely devoted to experiences with the DACA application process. Individuals share the duration of the application process, the reasons they were denied, and additional documents that are requested. He talks about his experiences and thoughts while wading through the application process:

> Yeah, I got approved in February. It was kind of like an up-and-down sort of process and I guess I applied in September and I got it in February, so roughly five months. In contrast, my brothers applied in October and got it in January, so it was kind of unnerving to know that people who applied after you were getting approved, so I was happy for them but at the same time I was kind of uneasy in that. Because I had this whole theory cooked up that because I could have been essentially

a person of interest to the United States or because I'm at the forefront of this whole thing [activist], that I may have been delayed because they were looking more into my application.

There are instances in which the U.S. Immigration and Customs Enforcement (ICE) targets the undocumented, for example, when the mother and brother of high-profile immigrant-rights activist Erika Andiola from Arizona were taken from their homes in the middle of the night. Such actions naturally create a sense of fear and cause undocumented individuals to act cautiously or experience a sense of paranoia, an element in the DACA application process that the Obama administration has completely ignored. For many of these participants, being DACAmented has various meanings that often hinge on their own legal consciousness. The next section discusses how the participants in this study make meaning of their DACAmented status.

DACA Does Not Equal Freedom

Once individuals receive their DACA status, they are given a Social Security number, allowing individuals (depending on the state they reside in) to apply for a driver's license, to open a bank account, and, in some states, to have the ability to pay in-state college tuition. Hours after he received his DACA card, Juan took to social media and tweeted, "I licked my card and it tastes like plastic, it doesn't taste like freedom," which is a common response to what DACA means: a temporary relief but not freedom. Yovany, from Georgia, also explains,

> I was telling my friend, it's like here, we won our freedom and we're giving our freedom away. So, like, oh wait, now they can know who I am and they can track me and so it's like not freedom, what is it? My freedom would be freedom to express yourself, freedom of right, freedom to do as you please and not to be offensive to anybody but I think the government shouldn't take your freedom here, even if you aren't a citizen. I don't know if freedom is even tangible.

The intention of DACA is to provide individuals with a work permit. More individuals working aids in improving the U.S. economic infrastructure. The conflict is that DACA recipients who are working are not afforded the same liberties as are others in the workforce. This structure creates a two-tiered class system of noncitizens. Most of the participants understand that the notion of "freedom" cannot be conceptualized if their family members are not able to reap the same benefits. Jorge, from Wisconsin, missed eligibility for DACA by one year and describes DACA as "having a blanket when your whole family is in the cold and you're the only one that has it." Not having equal benefits, rights, and safeties for other undocumented family members was the most common critique of the DACA policy, in addition to concerns about the future of activist work.

Fears of Complacency

There is no question that having DACA status offers an additional privilege to individuals living in the U.S. without long-term legal status. Despite these privileges, many of the participants in this study hope that DACA recipients understand that activism does not cease. Ariel, from Washington, expresses his sentiments:

> But I feel DACA was good, I think it's not a full option, I think there's certainly a lot of people who believe that now because of DACA, I think I told you before, people who believe that DACA happened and therefore that students are no longer going to be involved, that it doesn't matter, that there's people who are like, oh, well we got what we wanted, right, so now people have to go on their own. So I'm completely against that.

Yahaira also adds that while the fear of complacency does exist, there's also the question of how one uses this newfound privilege for the betterment of the immigration movement, "because otherwise, what's the point if you're not using it [DACA status] to leverage the work that they're [activists] doing."

Unlearning to Be Undocumented

Most interesting was hearing that there was a period of adjustment for some participants as they transitioned from being undocumented to being DACAmented. Juan eloquently pinpoints this process through his personal experiences about this adjustment:

> I don't know. It's kind of weird just on the sense that personally myself, I had to start the documents back in 2009 to some degree or another… . I think my work permit expired in 2009, my driver's license expired. So for the past five years, depending how you look at it, I have been without documents. And now that I think it's kind of like a two-way street the way that my mind is working. So like I know what having several documents feels like, so I'm thankful for it. To have, kind of none [of] the other sense, I'm trying to break out the psychological, having, holding back for the past couple years. I went through a transition period in the past couple of weeks since I've had this [DACA], I've noticed myself thinking things and I'm kind of like, whoa, that's silly. Like one night, for example, my parents were like, 'Oh, we're going to such and such's house for drinks, can you drive us?' And in my head I'm like, 'Oh my God, it's nine o'clock, it's late, are you going to be drinking, or what the hell.' So, you know, 15 seconds after I catch myself I'm like, oh, well, I have my driver's license so it doesn't matter as long as I don't drink. So that same occurrence happened to me, I would say three, or four, five times already… . I have been kind of indoctrinated to think that I'm not allowed to drive, that I should be scared of the police officers that are on the street and stuff like that. And it happens… . So it's kind of fascinating how this whole psychology works because at the end of the day you kind of realize how big of a part this whole undocumented mentality has weighed on you. Not because this whole undocumented unafraid persona but also because, in some way or another, you have been oppressed to a sense that you think that you are not unable to do these things with or without permission.

In many ways, becoming DACAmented is like assuming a new element of identity. The practices of living as undocumented individuals become ingrained in everyday lives so much so that they reconfigure how individuals learn to live with certain liberties. Evident in Juan's statement is how he has been conditioned to live within the confines of his legal status. His description eerily resembles imprisonment. While having a sense of agency to mold his life while accommodating his legal status, he has done so within a culture of surveillance. Operating under the watchful eye of the U.S. government has conditioned Juan to live his life carefully rather than carefree.

Applying Critical Legal Consciousness to DACA

It is important to note that most of the DACAmented recipients in this study felt grateful to have the benefits it affords them. However, many participants were privy to the political theater associated with the timing of this executive order, which coincided with the 2012 presidential election. While many of the participants became DACAmented during the course of this research study, a few expressed that they were not applying for DACA because they wanted to wait "to see what happens," or they wanted to explore other options. In Marco's case, he is resisting applying for DACA because his philosophical views are incongruent with the policy. During one of his removal proceedings, a judge indicated that if he applied for DACA, the court would halt his deportation proceedings. He refused and theorizes his decision by stating,

> So it's not to say that I don't believe in Deferred Action, but because I definitely do and I think people that benefit from it should do it because some people just can't afford to not provide for their families, and can't afford not to take it because I think just the opportunities that come with it are much better and I think could, again, bring relief to people and, again, to not undermine any form of any people's suffering. But I think then, yeah, to renounce it in court, I think we were trying to push back a little bit on it and be more inclusive about folks that can apply for Deferred Action, or like also pushing back against the narrative that we have asked forgiveness from a system that has wronged us…. I believe that, I mean we're like the last people to be blamed and then our parents also shouldn't be blamed because the systems that forced this upon us are to be blamed. So why should the reparation come from our end? So I think that's also what we're getting at and also getting at, the deeper than that is the injustices that occur within the immigration court, like the lack of, the absence of due process, and just the legal help, and the absence of fair and just trials, and just punishments that fit the crime…. I mean I think we are trying to open the spectrum for that to happen and try to be creative about it. So, hopefully, some of that'll happen and it just wasn't seen as not just an act of rebellion that was insubstantial.

Marco's sentiments ring true. As Americans, how often do we ask ourselves how our past foreign policies have created disastrous economic situations in neighboring countries? The intentions behind resisting

DACA are in response to the inhumane and terrorizing acts of the immigration system. Marco's critical legal consciousness focuses on challenging and interrogating the broader immigration system in order to unveil its injustices. Critical legally conscious activists understand that restoring justice through legalization of the 12 million undocumented immigrants is central to their discourse. They resist master narratives, which perpetuate the dichotomies of "undeserving and deserving" immigrants. They create counterstories of resistance by using their stories and narratives to illuminate an unjust immigration system. Critical legal consciousness is an epistemology in which undocumented immigrants not only view the world in radical ways, but they also create a life that allows them to live and act purposely, and with the intent of creating systemic change.

Reflections

Deferred Action for Childhood Arrivals (DACA) is a two-year temporary relief policy for those who qualify. Everyone in this study felt "cautiously optimistic" that DACA would lead to permanent action for the 12 million undocumented immigrants in the U.S. Currently, immigration reform has been stalled in Congress and the notion of putting people before politics is a farce. If indeed undocumented people were central to the immigration conversation, then placing a Band-Aid on the gushing immigration wound would not have been considered. Instead, there would have been a critical examination of the root causes of immigration and an investigation of the long-term consequences of not providing a pathway to citizenship for the 12 million undocumented individuals residing in the U.S. This policy appeases the mainstream masses by not teetering on the side of amnesty while giving eligible DACA recipients some "relief."

Using my own critical lens, I acknowledge that this policy does provide DACA-eligible individuals with some newfound privileges. However, I view DACA as a form of surveillance, a policy that perpetuates subservience, and as a systemic way to further subcategorize the undocumented population. The 600,000 DACAmented individuals residing in this country will learn to live in two-year increments. They will plan their entire lives around a two-year expiration date and new stressors associated with becoming and being DACAmented will emerge. In the end, providing legal status to the 12 million undocumented individuals residing in the U.S. would be the most humane option as DACA is considered "at best, a second-class status" (Gonzales, Terriquez, & Ruszczyk, 2014, p. 16). I refer to Jorge's words used to describe DACA as "having a blanket when your whole family is in the cold and you're the only one that has it." DACA potentially creates these divisions among families; amnesty provides families with a chance to live the life they choose.

Chapter Eight

Conclusion

I shook my head and took a deep sigh as I read the reviewer's comments out loud: "This research is biased and not everyone is going to agree with the legalization of illegal aliens." It stings, but over the years I've sadly been desensitized to these comments, especially from journal reviewers. I quickly craft a note to myself: "Isn't it our professional duty to assist all students in the best way possible, isn't it ethical to inform ourselves of issues and topics so that we can serve the needs of our students to the best of our abilities, and will undocumented students always be considered political pawns rather than college students?" I put aside my pink ballpoint pen and sigh again. I gaze outside my office window on to the newly tarred asphalt parking lot and think to myself, "I know better. I know that our country was founded on anti-immigrant values and institutional systems have been constructed to sustain these inequities. I know that most people will be stuck on 'Why couldn't they immigrate the "legal way"?' as a way to defend their stance on anti-immigration policies. I certainly know that, historically, oppressed individuals operate under a system which works against rather than for undocumented people. And I know there is fear within the higher education system that makes folks more comfortable staying silent about this issue. This civil rights issue will continue as long as we sustain systems of inequities."

The journey-stories of the undocumented and unafraid individuals in this study depict the experiences of millions of undocumented people residing in the U.S. While no one experience or journey toward understanding legality in an anti-immigration context is the same, the consequences, destruction, and challenges of living without legal status are relatively similar. The narratives in this study also highlight the complexity and fluidity of the ways in which study participants view their legal status within the context of other salient identities.

As I write the conclusion to this book, thousands of unaccompanied minors from Central America have crossed the U.S. border seeking refuge. This event has heightened fearmongering against undocumented immigrants. In a recent article, Rand Paul blames policies like DACA for the influx of children at the border saying, "The whole idea that the president unilaterally offered these areas of forgiveness for the kids—this DREAM kind of forgiveness—the problem is if you do that with an open border, then the whole world will come" (as quoted in Boyle, 2014, para. 2). Most problematic about this statement is the underlying assumption that undocumented ("DREAM" eligible) individuals have somehow "wronged" the American public, which warrants "forgiveness" from the U.S. These continuing fabrications are intended to position immigrants as villains, criminals, and lawbreakers, when in fact undocumented immigrants have not broken any criminal laws. Crossing the border without inspection or residing in the U.S. without documentation is a civil law infringement, equal in severity to traffic violations. In contrast, anti-immigration rhetoric continues to label undocumented immigrants as though they have committed the most heinous crimes. Unspoken are the crimes perpetrated on undocumented immigrants such as labor exploitation, abuse, and even wrongful death. Rarely do we see acknowledgment of the years of imperfection and sins committed by U.S. policies and actions leading to unimaginable corruption, dysfunction, violence, and poverty in Mexico and in Central American countries. Similar to the participants in this study, the children at the border have been displaced and pushed out by gangs and violence. It is the past wrongdoings of U.S. government policies that have placed children at our borders; thus, it is U.S. citizens who should be the apologetic ones.

The stories in this book illustrate how individuals in this study make meaning of what it means to be "undocumented and unafraid" in U.S. society through their lived experiences and how they process them. How undocumented individuals make meaning of their legal status is also informed by how mainstream America views undocumented immigrants. Yahaira's words, "we are not operating under the same system," ring loudly in my thoughts. While resisting master narratives of undocumented immigrants through activism, these community activists are grappling with their own identities, how to live their lives, and how to unpack the trauma and stressors of living inside and outside the margins of society. It is through introspection that undocumented individuals develop a critical legal consciousness wherein they interrogate the system that has assaulted them. I believe it is when undocumented individuals reach this point of critical legal consciousness that healing can occur.

The questions that I continue to wrestle with are: Can the American public accept the legalization of 12 million undocumented immigrants? Can institutions of higher education welcome undocumented students in more meaningful ways? In attempting to address my first question, I believe the country needs to ask itself, "What we are afraid of?" According to the Pew Research Center (Brown, 2014), the Latina/o population has surpassed whites in states such as New Mexico and California, with Texas, Florida, and Nevada forecasted to follow suit. Immigration into the U.S. has been decreasing for the past decade and U.S. births have been the primary source of population increase for Latinas/os (Brown, 2014). Regardless of these facts, mainstream America continues to conjure images of millions of immigrants crossing our borders. This argument also fuels the heightened militarization of cities along the border.

The root of my question is: How do we dismantle a system that has systemically terrorized people of color? Hate and racial inequities are historically embedded in the American fabric of life. Until the American public fully understands the root cause of why immigration continues to exist and how the U.S. is implicated in the immigration push-pull factors and the benefits for the U.S. infrastructure, immigrants will continue to be the scapegoat for the economic woes in the U.S. Immigration is not a crisis; it is a civil rights issue.

Recommendations

My second question attempts to address the issue of equity in higher education. On the surface, institutions of higher education have led efforts to make college more accessible for undocumented students. Jesuit colleges and universities have recently been in the limelight for their inclusiveness of undocumented students, aligning their actions with their institutional mission (Perry, 2014). The University of California system has also recently opened new DREAM Centers, hiring student personnel administrators to work specifically with undocumented college students. While tuition equity and resources for undocumented students are steps toward inclusion, full inclusion of undocumented students requires a deeper commitment. Inclusion of undocumented students enables access to the federal financial aid process. Considering the income levels of many undocumented parents, the cost of in-state tuition without state and/or federal aid does not constitute "college access."

Legal status also needs to be central to the equity and diversity discourse. Equity is not a buffet table at which one is allowed to pick and choose what to support and what to discard. Equity includes the voices of all who are marginalized and minoritized by U.S. society. Institutions of higher education must examine their own histories of exclusion and acknowledge that systems of higher education were not constructed with diversity, equity, and inclusion as priorities. By acknowledging instances of hate, colleges validate the voices of those harmed by institutional racism and xenophobia; then the healing process, trust building, and meaningful relationships can begin. I offer several recommendations for colleges and universities in the following section.

Recommendations for Higher Education

Higher education continues to struggle between ideologies. Should schools be a reflection of contemporary society, or should institutions try to consciously shape society? One recommendation is to provide professional development opportunities to train faculty and staff about the needs of undocumented students. Arizona State University offers the DREAMzone Ally Certificate Program (http://sts.asu.edu/ DREAMzone), which assists individuals as they develop ally competencies. These programs are instrumental in providing staff and faculty the language to engage in conversations about this topic. More important, it brings undocumented students from out of the shadows. The "don't ask, don't tell" policy that some colleges and universities employ further dehumanizes undocumented students, while college administrators contend that they are "protecting" the needs of undocumented students by not drawing attention to the issue. Participating in open and healthy dialogue about the needs of undocumented students on campus is a courageous step to take in addressing this civil rights issue.

Over the course of the past decade, college presidents have publically announced their support for undocumented students. I recommend that college presidents and university leaders not wait for comprehensive immigration reform to pass Congress, but instead initiate talks with stakeholders and policy makers about creating concrete policies to include undocumented students into the fabric of higher education. Higher education needs courageous leadership to encourage individuals to engage in uncomfortable dialogue. Courageous leadership is not about having a solution, but about taking the time to listen to the feedback of others while setting one's own personal beliefs aside. Courageous leadership is also about fostering open and transparent communication within the university community and leading change with humility and integrity. Including the needs of undocumented students in higher education strengthens the values and commitment around equity issues.

Colleges and universities should understand that social activism, or civil disobedience, is an arbitrary choice. The act of fighting for civil rights has leveraged these activists to find their purpose through involvement, access to resources, services, and community relationships that impact college persistence. Building meaningful relationships and trust with community entities (affiliates such as United We Dream, ScholarshipsA-Z, Voces de la Frontera, or DREAM Team) can be one way that higher education can impact college access and student persistence. These intentional partnerships can be a source of knowledge and alliance for college administrators seeking to understand the pressing needs of undocumented youth within their local context. For example, college administrators can use community organizations for staff professional development. I encourage intentional relationship building with community college advisors who work specifically with undocumented students. College advisors should provide college application assistance in community entity spaces. In return, an authentic alliance with these entities would ensure their use of campus space, technology, and other resources to provide knowledge concerning undocumented students. Faculty can also establish an advocacy group such as an "Immigration Scholars Council," which could help leverage the needs of undocumented students in faculty assembly and other academic spaces. Faculty and staff can also work with development officers to raise funds for scholarships for undocumented students.

Recommendations for K–12 Teachers

One teacher has the power to validate a student. Teachers and school administrators need seamless partnerships with community entities. For instance, by conducting a professional development conference for teachers and school leaders, community entities are able to disseminate resources related to working with undocumented students, and assist in the college access process. Teachers should also encourage students to form high school advocacy groups (DREAM clubs) for undocumented students as well as allies. Documented students are also able to inform themselves about the needs of undocumented students so that they can offer peer support. I also recommend that schools develop strategic plans around establishing family outreach for undocumented students.

Recommendations for Student Identity Theories

I teach a course called "Students in the Collegiate Context" that reviews foundational student development theories used to inform practice and research. While many strides have been made to address the shortcomings and lack of attention to race, class, and gender, every year one student asks, "Where are the student development theories addressing the needs of undocumented students?" I recommend that student affairs practitioners employ the notion of interrogation of legal status and legal consciousness within the student development theory context. By understanding the influences and strategies with which students navigate their legal status, college campuses can build supportive mechanisms to foster not only future exploration of their identities, but also how retention and graduation efforts can be inclusive of factors impacting students without legal status. The meaning-making process of one's legal consciousness is an emotional, introspective, and challenging journey, one that requires time and an adequate support system.

I highly encourage college administrators and higher education faculty members to consider legal status as a social identity and to be inclusive of this subpopulation in their policies, scholarship, and practice. Neglecting to include undocumented students in the fabric of our educational systems implicates us as oppressors.

Recommendations for Research Ethics

As a researcher of students without documentation living in the U.S., I grapple time and time again with my own privilege and power. I acknowledge the power differentials between the participants and myself in this study and continually questioned how to dismantle these power dynamics within my research. I knew that I did not want to become a "commuter researcher" (Elise & Umoja, 1992; Mahalingam & Rabelo, 2013), a researcher who does not have social connections with the immigrant community and has not built substantive relationships to further enhance his or her worldview or knowledge. I recommend that researchers engaging in studying immigrants or other minoritized populations answer the following two questions: Why do you do this work? What positive impact do you hope your work will make in the immigrant community? Grappling and struggling with one's privilege is an important ethical responsibility when conducting just social research.

An Open Letter to Undocumented Student Activists

Dear Immigration Youth Activists:

After the last edit has been submitted, after each reference is correctly cited, after all my typos and grammatical errors are rectified, this book will go on to be published. I do not claim that this book will be perfect and hope that you can find the beauty in these imperfections. I acknowledge that there are many voices that are not included in this book, different perspectives and ethnicities. You may even find yourself disagreeing with what is written in this book. I am okay with this. The intent of this book is to acknowledge the multiplicity and fluidity associated with what it means to be undocumented and unafraid and how migration experiences, context, and personal growth aid the developmental process of these identities. With each new beginning, context, and person who enters your life, you are changed, just like the journey-stories of the undocumented community activists in this book have left their footprints on my heart.

The activists in this book have helped me to reconsider my role in the professorate. Why do I do this work? It pleased me greatly that some of the participants were diligent about asking me what I was going to do with the research. They would ask, "How are you going to make sure that this information gets into our community rather than just keeping it among your academic culture?" This is a tremendous question, one that challenges me to look at my research from an activist, feminist, and critical lens, particularly when value is placed on publishing in mainstream academic journals that make access to scholarship and research virtually inaccessible to youthful communities of color. While the academy continues to be an uncomfortable space for critical race work, I find support and encouragement among a small group of scholars who are also studying undocumented youth.

This book was by far the most difficult writing endeavor of my entire academic career. The challenge was not in enduring long bouts of writing sessions (my dissertation prepared me for that task) nor in the time associated with coding and analyzing the hundreds of pages of transcriptions. My dilemma during this book writing process was constantly questioning whether I was honoring and representing the voices of the participants in a way that does justice to their plights as undocumented individuals living in U.S. society. I feared disappointing the individuals in this book or other undocumented students. After reaching out to mentors, I now realize that my fear stems from a place of love and care for a community that has gifted me more than I could have asked for. Another unexpected hurdle were my own emotions surrounding the data collection and writing process. I am utterly humbled that the participants in this book were so candid and forthright about their experiences, which allowed me to peek into their souls. I did not expect the flood of tears as a result of having to analyze and write around the pain, trauma, injustices, and struggles experienced by the individuals in this book. Once these narratives are read, the reader becomes implicated in these injustices and is forced to reflect on his or her own position with respect to this issue.

Throughout this research project, I thought about the parents and families of undocumented community activists. Families are pillars of strength, and I recognize the important role that parents play in why you, the undocumented activist, are currently engaged in activist work. I also acknowledge that certain liberties and freedoms were taken from you and your families as a result of your journeys and lived experiences in the U.S. I honor the plight of and the decisions made by families to reside in the U.S. for a better life. Their choice to leave family and country of origin probably came with much deliberation and anxiety. As a mother of two girls, there is no doubt that I would climb over walls of fire to make sure that they were safe and that they are afforded the best opportunities available.

Those of us who are immigrants in this country stand on the shoulders of parents. Our parents had enough courage, conviction, and will to make that trek to the U.S., leaving behind people, possessions, and a country that they once called home to give us a better life. Critics are quick to blame parents who only wanted a chance at survival, a just and moral act. To deny one's child a better life would be unjust. I also acknowledge that many undocumented immigrants come to the U.S. with documentation but because of the backlog, the complex bureaucracy, and, in some cases, the fraudulent actions taken by U.S. lawyers, the expiration date of visas caused families to live without status.

While this research is based on these specific undocumented community activists, we must recognize that the parents of these activists work the earth for crops to sprout, they wake up at the crack of dawn to prepare amenities for our workplaces and hotels, and they labor long hours for degrading wages. We must recognize that immigrant workers residing in the U.S. also need legalization.

Finally, I do not claim to speak for undocumented immigrants. You are MORE than capable of speaking on your own behalf. Undocumented and documented immigrants have always possessed an enormous amount of assets, knowledge, self-agency, and perseverance. However, the controlling images of immigrants form a different picture. There are strength, love, and imperfection within the undocumented youth movement. I am an outsider looking in, I have legal status privilege, and I stand as an ally with the undocumented youth movement. The mere fact that you have helped shape the immigration discourse in the U.S. and transformed higher education and federal policies establishes you as part of American history.

Bibliography

Abes, E. S. (2009). Theoretical borderlands: Using multiple theoretical perspectives to challenge inequitable power structures in student development theory. *Journal of College Student Development, 50,* 141–156. doi:10.1353/csd.0.0059

Abes, E. S., Jones, S. R., & McEwen, M. K. (2007). Reconceptualizing the Model of Multiple Dimensions of Identity: The role of meaning-making capacity in the construction of multiple identities. *Journal of College Student Development, 48,* 1–22.

Abrego, L. (2011). Legal consciousness of undocumented Latinos: Fear and stigma as barriers to claims making for first and 1.5 generation immigrants. *Law & Society Review, 45*(2), 337–369.

Alabama House Bill 56. (2011). Beason-Hammon Alabama Taxpayer and Citizen Protection Act.

Alcoff, L. (2006). *Visible identities: Race, gender, and the self.* Oxford: Oxford University Press.

Alemán, E., Jr., Delgado Bernal, D., & Mendoza, S. (2013). Critical race methodological tensions: Nepantla in our community-based praxis. In M. Lynn & A. Dixson (Eds.). *Handbook for critical race theory in education* (pp. 325–338). New York, NY: Routledge.

Anzaldúa, G. (1987). *Borderlands/La frontera: The new mestiza.* San Francisco, CA: Aunt Lute Books.

Anzaldúa, G. (1999). *Borderlands/La frontera: The new mestiza* (2nd ed.). San Francisco, CA: Aunt Lute Books.

Aranda, E. M., & Rebollo-Gil, G. (2004). Ethnoracism and the "sandwiched" minorities. *American Behavioral Scientist, 47*(7), 910–927. doi:10.1177/0002764203261071

Arizona Senate Bill 1070. (2010). Support Our Law Enforcement and Safe Neighborhoods Act. Retrieved from http://www.scotusblog.com/wp-content/uploads/2010/07/DOJ-AZ-brief-7-6-10.pdf

Barrera, D. (2011, November 27). Student commits suicide, letters reveal worries over immigration status. *KGBT 4 News*. Retrieved at http://www.valleycentral.com/news/story.aspx?id=690993#.VLL9kFupr0s

Bohon, S. A., Macpherson, H., & Atiles, J. H. (2005). Educational barriers for new Latinos in Georgia. *Journal of Latinos and Education, 4*(1), 43–58. doi:10.1207/s1532771xjle0401_4

Brown, A. (2014, June 26). *U.S. Hispanic and Asian populations growing, but for different reasons*. Retrieved from Pew Research Center website: http://www.pewresearch.org/fact-tank/2014/06/26/u-s-hispanic-and-asian-populations-growing-but-for-different-reasons/

Bstewart23. (2008, November 22). Harvey Implores [Video file]. Retrieved from https://www.youtube.com/watch?v=UvZIoZNYTN8#t=29

Butler, J. (1993a). Imitation and gender insubordination. In H. Abelove, M. A. Barale & D. M. Halperin (eds), *The lesbian and gay studies reader* (pp. 307–320). New York; London: Routledge.

Butler, J. (1993b). *Bodies that matter: On the discursive limits of sex*. New York: Routledge.

Bulter-Flora, J., & Maldonado, M. (2006). Immigrants as assets for midwestern communities. *Changing Faces. 12*(4). Retrieved from http://migration.ucdavis.edu/cf/more.php?id=190_0_2_0

Chang, A. (2011). Undocumented to hyperdocumented: A jornada of protection, papers, and PhD status. *Harvard Educational Review, 81*(3), 508–521.

Chavez, L. (2008). *The Latino threat: Constructing immigrants, citizens, and the nation*. Redwood City, CA: Stanford University Press.

Chavez, M. L., Soriano, M., & Oliverez, P. (2007). Undocumented students' access to college: The American dream denied. *Latino Studies, 5*(2), 254–263.

Chickering, A. W., & Reisser, L. (1993). *Education and identity* (2nd ed.). San Francisco, CA: Jossey-Bass.

Coleman, E. (1982). Developmental stages of the coming out process. *Journal of homosexuality, 7*(2-3), 31–43. doi:10.1177/1359104597023005

Collins, P. H. (1990). *Black feminist thought*. New York: Routledge.

Corrunker, L. (2012). "Coming out of the shadows": DREAM Act activism in the context of global anti-deportation activism. *Indiana Journal of Global Legal Studies, 19*(1), 143–168.

Cox, N., Dewaele, A., Van Houtte, M., & Vincke, J. (2010). Stress-related growth, coming out, and internalized homonegativity in lesbian, gay, and bisexual youth. An examination of stress-related growth within the minority stress model. *Journal of Homosexuality, 58*(1), 117–137. doi:10.1080/00918369.2011.533631

Crenshaw, K. (1991). Mapping the margins: Intersectionality, identity politics, and violence against women of color. *Stanford Law Review, 43*(6), 1241–1299.

Crotty, M. (2003). *The foundations of social research: Meaning and perspective in the research process*. Thousand Oaks, CA: Sage.

Dalgin, R. S., & Gilbride, D. (2003). Perspectives of people with psychiatric disabilities on employment disclosure. *Psychiatric Rehabilitation Journal, 26*(3), 306–301.

De Genova, N. (2002). Migrant "illegality" and deportability in everyday life. *Annual Review of Anthropology, 31*, 419–447. doi: 10.1146/annurev.anthro.31.040402.085432

De Genova, N. (2005). *Working the boundaries: Race, space, and "illegality" in Mexican Chicago*. Durham, NC: Duke University Press.

De Genova, N., & Ramos-Zayas, A. Y. (2003). *Latino crossings: Mexicans, Puerto Ricans, and the politics of race and citizenship*. New York: Routledge.

Deaux, K. (1993). Reconstruction social identity. *Personality and Social Psychology Bulletin, 19*(1), 4–12. doi: 10.1177/0146167293191001

Drachman, E. (2006). Access to higher education for undocumented students. *Peace Review, 18*(1), 91–100. doi: 10.1080/10402650500511667

DREAM Act. (2010, November 18). Retrieved from http://www.immigrationpolicy.org/just-facts/dream-act

DREAM Act of 2001, Pub. L No. 104–208, § 952 (2001).

Drop the I-word. (n.d.). Retrieved from http://colorlines.com/droptheiword/

Elise, S., & Umoja, A. (1992). Spike Lee constructs the New Black man: Mo' better. *The Western Journal of Black Studies, 16*(2), 82–89.

Ellis, L. M., & Chen, E. C. (2013). Negotiating identity development among undocumented immigrant college students: A grounded theory study. *Journal of Counseling Psychology, 60*(2), 251–264. doi: 10.1037/a0031350

Enriquez, L. E. (2014). "Undocumented and citizen students unite" building a cross-status coalition through shared ideology. *Social Problems, 61*(2), 155–174.

Erikson, E. H. (1968). *Identity, youth, and crisis*. New York: W. W. Norton.

Fairfield University, Loyola University Chicago, Santa Clara University Legal and Social Research Teams. (2013). *Immigrant student national position paper executive summary* [Executive Summary]. Retrieved from http://www.fairfield.edu/media/fairfield universitywebsite/documents/academic/cfpl_immigration_summary.pdf

Flores, S., & Chapa, J. (2009). Latino immigrant access to higher education in a bipolar context of reception. *Journal of Hispanic Higher Education, 8*(1), 90–109. doi: 10.1177/1538192708326996

Galindo, R. (2012). Undocumented & unafraid: The DREAM Act 5 and the public disclosure of undocumented status as a political act. *The Urban Review, 44*(5), 589–611. doi:10.1007/s11256-012-0219-0

Galván, R. (2006). Campesina epistemologies and pedagogies of the spirit: Examining women's sobrevivencia. In D. Delgado Bernal, C. A. Elenes, F. E. Godinez, & S. Villenas (Eds.), *Chicana/Latina education in everyday life: Feminista perspectives on pedagogy and epistemology* (pp. 161–179). Albany: State University of New York Press.

Garcia, A. M. (1989). The development of Chicana feminist discourse, 1970–1980. *Gender & Society, 3*(2), 217–238.

Garcia, L. (2013). *Undocumented and unwanted: Attending college against the odds.* New York: LFB Scholarly Publishing.

Gildersleeve, R. E. (2010). *Fracturing opportunity: Mexican migrant students and college going literacy.* New York: Peter Lang Publishing.

Gómez-Quinones, J., & Vásquez, I. (2014). *Making Aztlan: Ideology and culture of the Chicana and Chicano movement, 1966–1977.* Albuquerque, NM: University of New Mexico Press.

Gonzales, R. G. (2008). Left out but not shut down: Political activism and the undocumented student movement. *Northwestern Journal of Law and Social Policy, 3*(21), 219–239.

Gonzales, R. G. (2011). Learning to be illegal: Undocumented youth and shifting legal contexts in the transition to adulthood. *American Sociological Review, 76*(4), 602–619. doi: 10.1177/0003122411411901

Gonzales, R. G., & Bautista Chavez, A. M. (2014). *Two years and counting: Assessing the growth and power of DACA. American Immigration Council* (Report). Retrieved from American Immigration Council website: http://www.immigrationpolicy. org/sites/default/files/docs/two_years_and_counting_assessing_the_growing_ power_of_daca_final.pdf

Gonzales, R. G., & Chavez, L. R. (2012). Awakening to a nightmare: Abjectivity and illegality in the lives of undocumented 1.5 generation Latino immigrants in the United States. *Current Anthropology, 53*(3), 255–281.

Gonzales, R. G., & Terriquez, V. (2013, August 15). *How DACA is impacting the lives of those who are now DACAmented: Preliminary findings from the national UnDACAmented Research Project* (Report). Retrieved from American Immigration Council website: http://www.immigrationpolicy.org/just-facts/how-daca-impacting-lives-those-who-are-now-dacamented

González, F. E. (1999). Formations of "Mexicana"ness: Trenzas de identidades multiples [Growing up Mexicana: Braids of multiple identities]. In L. Parker, D. Deyhle, & S. Villenas (Eds.), *Race is ... race isn't: Critical race theory and qualitative studies in education* (pp. 156–172). Boulder, CO: Perseus.

Grey, M. A., & Woodrick, A. C. (2005). Latinos have revitalized our community: Mexican migration and Anglo responses in Marshalltown, Iowa. In V. Zúñiga & R. Hernández-León (Eds.), *New destinations: Mexican immigration in the United States* (pp. 133–154). New York: Russell Sage Foundation.

Grosfoguel, R. (2004). Race and ethnicity or racialized ethnicities. *Ethnicities, 4*(3), 315–336. doi: 0.1177/1468796804045237

Gutierrez, D. G. (1991). "Sin Fronteras?": Chicanos, Mexican Americans, and the emergence of the contemporary Mexican immigration debate, 1968–1978. *Journal of American Ethnic History,* 5–37.

Hardiman, R., & Jackson, B. W., III. (1997). Conceptual foundation for social justice course. In M. Adams, L. A. Bell, & P. Griffin (Eds.), *Teaching for diversity and social justice: A sourcebook* (pp. 16–29). New York: Routledge.

Hossler, D., Braxton, J., & Coopersmith, G. (1989). Understanding student college choice. In J. C. Smart (Ed.), *Higher education: Handbook of theory and research* (Vol. 4). New York: Agathon.

Hossler, D., & Gallagher, K. S. (1987). Studying college choice: A three-phase model and the implication for policy makers. *College and University, 2*(3), 207–221.

Hossler, D., Schmit, J., & Vesper, N. (1999). *Going to college: How social, economic, and educational factors influence the decisions students make.* Baltimore, MD: Johns Hopkins University Press.

Jensen, L. (2006). New immigrant settlements in rural America: Problems, prospects, and polices. *Reports on Rural America, 1*(3), 1–34. Retrieved from http://scholars.unh.edu/cgi/viewcontent.cgi?article=1016&context=carsey

Jones, S. R., & Abes, E. S. (2013). *Identity development of college students: Advancing frameworks for multiple dimensions of identity.* San Francisco, CA: Jossey-Bass Publishing.

Jones, S. R., & McEwen, M. K. (2000). A conceptual model of multiple dimensions of identity. *Journal of College Student Development, 41*, 405–414. doi:10.1353/csd.2007.0000

Josselson, R. (1987). *Finding herself: Pathway to identity development in women.* San Francisco, CA: Jossey-Bass.

Kohli, R., & Solórzano, D. G. (2012). Teachers, please learn our names!: Racial microaggressions and the K-12 classroom. *Race Ethnicity and Education, 15*(4), 441–462. doi: 10.1080/13613324.2012.674026

Mahalingam, R., & Rabelo, V. C. (2013). Theoretical, methodological, and ethical challenges to the study of immigrants: Perils and possibilities. In M. G. Hernandez, J. Nguyen, C. L. Saetermoe, & C. Suarez-Orozco (Eds.), *Frameworks and Ethics for Research with Immigrants: New Directions for Child and Adolescent Development, 141,* 25–41.

Maldonado, M. M., & Licona, A. C. (2007). Re-thinking integration as reciprocal and spatialized process. *Journal of Latino/Latin American Studies, 2*(4), 128–43.

Manning, J. (2014). Communicating sexual identities: A typology of coming out. *Sexuality & Culture,* 1–17. doi: 10.1007/s12119-014-9251-4

Marcia, J. W. (1966). Developing and validation of ego-identity status. *Journal of Personality and Social Psychology, 3*, 551–558.

McDonough, P. M. (1998). *Choosing colleges: How social class and schools structure opportunity.* Albany: State University of New York Press.

Menjívar, C., & Abrego, L. (2012). Legal violence: Immigration law and the lives of Central American immigrants. *American Journal of Sociology, 117*(5), 1380–1421.

Muñoz, C. (1989). *Youth, identity, power: The Chicano movement.* New York: Verso.

Muñoz, S. M., & Maldonado, M. M. (2011). Counterstories of college persistence by undocumented Mexicana students: Navigating race, class, gender, and legal status. *International Journal of Qualitative Studies in Education*, 1–23. doi: 10.1080/09518398.2010.529850

Negrón-Gonzales, G. (2014). Undocumented, unafraid and unapologetic: Re-articulatory practices and migrant youth "illegality." *Latino Studies, 12*(2), 259–278. doi: 10.1057/lst.2014.20

Nevarez, G. (2014, September 18). Dolores Huerta says Obama made the right decision on deportation relief. *The Huffington Post*. Retrieved from http://www.huffingtonpost.com/2014/09/18/dolores-huerta-obama-immigration_n_5845798.html

Nicholls, W. J. (2013). *The DREAMers: How the undocumented youth movement transformed the immigration rights debate*. Stanford, CA: Stanford University Press.

Nicholls, W. J. (2014). From political opportunities to niche-openings: The dilemmas of mobilizing for immigrant rights in inhospitable environments. *Theory and Society, 43*(1). 23–49. doi: 10.1007/s11186-013-9208-x

Oboler, S. (1995). *Ethnic labels, Latino lives: Identity and the politics of (re)presentation in the United States*. Minneapolis: University of Minnesota Press.

Olivas, M. A. (2012). *No undocumented child left behind*: Plyler v. Doe *and the education of undocumented schoolchildren*. New York: New York University Press.

Orgad, L., & Ruthizer, T. (2010). Race, religion, and nationality in immigration selection 120 years after the Chinese exclusion case. *Constitution Commentary, 12*, 110–153.

Orne, J. (2011). "You will always have to 'out' yourself": Reconsidering coming out through strategic outness. *Sexualities, 14*(6), 681–703.

Patton, L. D. (2011). Perspectives on identity, disclosure and the campus environment among African American gay and bisexual men at one historically Black college. *Journal of College Student Development, 52*(1), 77–100.

Patton, L. D., McEwen, M., Rendón, L., & Howard-Hamilton, M. F. (2007). Critical race perspectives on theory in student affairs. *New Directions for Student Services, 2007*(120), 39–53.

Patton, M. (2002). *Qualitative research and evaluation methods* (3rd ed.). Thousand Oaks, CA: Sage.

Pérez, P. A. (2010). College choice process of Latino undocumented students: Implications for recruitment and retention. *Journal of College Admission, 206*, 21–25.

Pérez, P. A., & McDonough, P. M. (2008). Understanding Latina and Latino college choice: A social capital and chain migration analysis. *Journal of Hispanic Higher Education, 7*(3), 249–265.

Pérez, W. (2011). *Americans by heart: Undocumented Latino students and the promise of higher education*. New York: Teachers College Press.

Pérez Huber, L. (2009). Challenging racist nativist framing: Acknowledging the community cultural wealth of undocumented Chicana college students to reframe the immigration debate. *Harvard Educational Review, 79*(4), 704–730.

Pérez Huber, L. (2010). Using Latina/o critical race theory and racist nativism to explore intersectionality in the educational experiences of undocumented Chicana college students. *Educational Foundations, 24*(1), 77–96.

Perry, D. A. (2014, July 21). Should colleges help undocumented students? A look at why many Catholic institutions are doing just that. *Chronicle of Higher Education.* Retrieved from http://chronicle.com/article/Should-Colleges-Help/147809

Plyler v. Doe, 457 U.S. 202 (1982).

Poindexter, C. C., & Shippy, R. A. (2010). HIV diagnosis disclosure: Stigma management and stigma resistance. *Journal of Gerontological Social Work, 53*(4), 366–381. doi: 10.1080/0163437

Portes, A., & Rumbaut, R. G. (2006). *Immigrant America: A portrait* (3rd ed.). Berkeley, CA: University of California Press.

Ragins, B. R., Singh, R., & Cornwell, J. M. (2007). Making the invisible visible: Fear and disclosure of sexual orientation at work. *Journal of Applied Psychology, 92*(4), 1103.

Said, E. W. (1993). *Culture and imperialism.* New York: Knopf.

Sandoval, C. (2000). *Methodology of the oppressed.* Minneapolis: University of Minnesota Press.

Sarlin, B. (2013, December 16). How America's harshest immigration law failed. *MSNBC News.* Retrieved from http://www.msnbc.com/msnbc/undocumented-workers-immigration-alabama

Seif, H. (2011). "Unapologetic and unafraid": Immigration youth come out of the shadows. In C. A. Flanagan & B. D. Christens (Eds.), *Youth Civic Development: Work at the Cutting Edge. New Directions for Child and Adolescent Development, 134,* 59–75.

Silbey, S. S. (2005). After legal consciousness. *Annual Review of Law and Social Science, 1*(1), 323–368. doi: 10.1146/annurev.lawsocsci.1.041604.115938

Solórzano, D., Ceja, M., & Yosso, T. (2000). Critical race theory, racial microaggressions, and campus racial climate: The experiences of African American college students. *Journal of Negro Education, 69*(1–2), 60–73.

Southern Poverty Law Center (2008). *Hate Crimes: Anti-Latino hate crime up for fourth year* (Report No. 132). Retrieved from http://www.splcenter.org/get-informed/intelligence-report/browse-all-issues/2008/winter/hate-crimes

Stanton-Salazar, R. D. (2011). A social capital framework for the study of institutional agents and their role in the empowerment of low-status students and youth. *Youth & Society, 43*(3), 1066–1109. doi: 10.1177/0044118x10382877

Suárez-Orozco, C., & Suárez-Orozco, M. (2001). *Children of immigration.* Cambridge, MA: Harvard University Press.

Sullivan, M. M., & Rehm, R. (2005). Mental health of undocumented Mexican immigrants: A review of the literature. *Advances in Nursing Science, 28*(3), 240–251. doi: 10.1097/00012272-200507000-00006

The DREAM Act: A resource page. (2010, September 16). Retrieved from http://www.immigrationpolicy.org/just-facts/dream-act-resource-page

Torres, V., Jones, S. R., & Renn, K. A. (2009). Identity development among theories in student affairs: Origins, current status, and new approaches. *Journal of College Student Development, 50*(6), 577–596. doi: 10.1353/csd.0.0102

U.S. Citizenship and Immigration Services. (2014, December 12). Consideration of deferred action for childhood arrivals. Retrieved from http://www.uscis.gov/humanitarian/consideration-deferred-action-childhood-arrivals-daca

Valverde, L. A. (2006). *Improving schools for Latinos: Creating better learning environments.* Lanham, MD: Rowman & Littlefield.

Villenas, S. A. (2005). Commentary: Latina literacies in convivencia. *Anthropology Education Quarterly, 36*(3), 273–277. doi:10.1525/aeq.2005.36.3.273

Yolanda Medina and Ángeles Donoso Macaya
GENERAL EDITORS

Critical Studies of Latinos/as in the Americas is a provocative interdiscipli-
nary series that offers a critical space for reflection and questioning what it
means to be Latino/a living in the Americas in twenty-first century social,
cultural, economic, and political arenas. The series looks forward to extend-
ing the dialogue to include the North and South Western hemispheric rela-
tions that are prevalent in the field of global studies.

Topics that explore and advance research and scholarship on contemporary topics and issues related with processes of racialization, economic exploitation, health, education, transnationalism, immigration, gendered and
sexual identities, and disabilities that are not commonly highlighted in the
current Latino/a Studies literature as well as the multitude of socio, cultural,
economic, and political progress among the Latinos/as in the Americas are
welcome.

To receive more information about CSLA, please contact:

Yolanda Medina (ymedina@bmcc.cuny.edu) &
Ángeles Donoso Macaya (mdonosomacaya@bmcc.cuny.edu)

To order other books in this series, please contact our Customer
Service Department at:

(800) 770-LANG (within the U.S.)
(212) 647-7706 (outside the U.S.)
(212) 647-7707 FAX

Or browse online by series at:

WWW.PETERLANG.COM